Lent 2000

ALL TOGETHER NOW

Exploring the Journey of Faith in Words and Music

CTBI
Inter-Church House
35-41 Lower Marsh
London SE1 7RL

ISBN 0 85169 249 4

©1999 Churches Together in Britain and Ireland
Published by CTBI
Inter-Church House
35-41 Lower Marsh
London SE1 7RL

Cover Design by Mark Whitchurch, Art & Design

Printed by Design & Print (Sussex) Ltd, Portslade, Brighton

Contents

PREFACE BY CTBI PRESIDENTS

Shared Lenten Study Groups have proved to be important in bringing Christians Together. *All Together Now* offers a new and imaginative way for local groups not only to explore their faith but to enjoy its expression, in this Year of Jubilee, in hymns and songs both old and new. In Lent 2000 we can both celebrate our diversity and sing together as one.

As Presidents of Churches Together in Britain and Ireland we warmly commend this Lent 2000 Course to local churches together. It is a study **using** hymns and songs rather than a study **about** hymns and songs. As we listen, sing and reflect together, we shall enter more fully into the joys and sorrows of our common faith, explore the issues they raise, and deepen our mutual understanding.

We are grateful to the Lent 2000 Planning Group for its work which CTBI is sponsoring in association with the national ecumenical bodies. We are sure that *All Together Now* will make a significant contribution to our celebrations at the start of the new millennium, following on from *Celebrating Unity in Prayer* in January, and looking forward to *Pentecost 2000*.

Rt Rev Mario Conti

Rt Rev Barry Rogerson

Rev Nezlin Sterling

Sister Eluned Williams

Presidents of Churches Together in Britain and Ireland

4

INTRODUCTION

I   Background and Pattern of the Course

'All Together Now'

Welcome! We hope this guide will be an inspirational companion and a useful tool during Lent 2000 and at other times of the year. The theme this year is *Exploring the Journey of Faith in Words and Music*. This material is devised for use by small and large groups and uses the medium of words and music, in songs and hymns, to explore the journey of faith. The pattern of *All Together Now* follows the simple pattern of the cycle of life, based on Gospel readings. The weeks lead us from BEGINNINGS through FOLLOWING, CHALLENGING, BELIEVING to DYING. The life-cycle of a human being, a congregation, a community or a limited company touches on all or some of these themes. And yet there is more. Dying is not the end of the story. Our Easter faith assures us that beyond death there is new life, there is healing, there is resurrection. But first we must travel through death to discover this new life. This simple pattern throws out a great challenge to us, to our churches and to our communities - how can we learn to die in order to have new life?

Lent 2000

While 2000 is a year of celebration, it can also be an opportunity to engage in issues and concerns which are important for many during Lent. Traditional Lenten themes are *prayer:* taking time alone and with others to reflect and meditate on issues of life and faith; *fasting:* re-considering the amount of food and material goods we consume; *giving* to those in need; *forgiving* others; *reaffirming* our sense of belonging and identity as Christians or as faith explorers. These Lenten themes, involving a fresh start in the eyes of our neighbours and of God, or turning around from old ways and looking for new ways to live in justice and peace in the world, are resonant with biblical themes of Jubilee. They are themes and issues which have radical implications for our lives and for the life of our world that will take us into 2000 and beyond.

The Focus: Words and Music

This material is for everyone. The focus is on sharing our faith and not on perfecting a choral piece or a choir anthem. It may be that music, hymns, worship and other songs play a very important part in your life and faith, in which case you may find new and challenging pieces here. If music does not feature strongly in your journey of faith, perhaps the themes presented here will touch you in new and unexpected ways. Whether you consider yourself to be 'musical' or not, we hope that you will be touched by the tenderness of some of the pieces and shaken by the passion of others. This is our aim. Enjoy the music and sing your heart out!

Wherever we go there is music in our culture, from the muzak which is funnelled through loud-speakers in shopping malls to nursery rhymes sung lustily by a toddler, to the best of the pop tradition and the finest string quartet or opera.

Music was used from very early times as a means of sharing the faith with those who could not read but knew how to sing a psalm. Indeed the psalms are often referred to as the song book of the people of Israel. The psalms would have been known and sung by Jesus and his contemporaries, and have been sung in many different settings and cultures throughout the world. Singing, and music can express the heart of our Christian faith.

For many, music is more than simply a tool to communicate the faith: music itself is an expression of faith. But in combining words with music we praise God; communicate our vision and faith; express our yearnings and our sorrows; build a sense of community together; encourage others to join with us on the journey of faith. Through music, hymns and worship songs we can encounter others in the various faith traditions in a way that transcends differences and touches on our common beliefs. But while music can bind us together across denominations, languages and cultures, music can also divide us. So we hope that through taking part in *All Together Now* we can each learn something from the traditions and tastes of others.

Choosing our Words Carefully

It is very difficult to know what one word to use when describing a range of musical items. Across the denominations there are many musical forms which use the voice, including chant, litany, hymn, processional song, psalm, worship song, spiritual and acclamation. Examples of all of these are offered in this course. In each case they combine music and text. But should we call them all hymns, songs, worship items? In the west, since the time of Martin Luther, the hymn has tended to be the foremost musical form used in communal worship. But what do we mean by 'hymn'? There are many definitions, but no single definitive understanding. A hymn could be described as a poetic composition which expresses experience and the Christian mystery, composed to be sung in a liturgical setting to a repeated tune for public worship. Usually a hymn is self-standing and is not tied to any particular liturgical rite eg a procession or a prayer. This would make the hymn different from litanies, psalms and processional songs, which set the Scriptures to music and have a specific role within the liturgy. Hymns were particularly popular in the Protestant

6

Churches. In the Catholic Church the hymn came into popular use in the Mass after Vatican II (1960s) with the use of the vernacular in worship.

However, there are other Christian traditions which would describe their musical items as worship songs (the common expression of a like-minded group in a popular, though not necessarily contemporary, idiom), others as litanies (prayers set to music for use in specific sections of worship), others simply as songs (which could refer to a completely secular song or to a piece of music with words that is given a specifically religious significance.)

In the course of this text a variety of words are used to describe the material. If this encourages discussion about terminology then so much the better.

Music

Some hymns and songs use music from the folk tradition or tunes that are well known for other reasons. In the oral tradition a ballad would be sung and learned, adapted, changed and then sung again. The folk tradition is a dynamic, fluid one, with messages being passed on from generation to generation in language that is adapted for the period. Similarly in hymnody and song-writing many writers have employed this technique, and have given new words to insights and beliefs that are very old, setting these words to well known tunes. In your group there may be some who are used to this style and like it and others who do not. It may be useful, where appropriate, to air some of these feelings. Perhaps there are some in your group who would feel encouraged to write their own songs or to compose new words to a well-known tune.

Language in Hymnody

Many of the hymns which we still love are written in language which speaks of men and sons etc when we also mean women and daughters. In the last twenty years it has become increasingly recognised in the church that such language is not acceptable. As the new Methodist Worship Book (February 1999) states 'Inclusive language is now regarded as normative; you can't get away with saying 'men' when you mean 'men, women and children'.' As a result when we have chosen hymns which originally spoke of 'men' and 'sons' we have used texts from hymn books where agreed changes have been made. If you have views on this, then you might like to raise them in your group.

Most of the hymns we sing regularly refer to God as Father or Lord or Almighty. In more recent times there has been a desire expressed for more language to describe God which draws on a wider range of biblical imagery and also refers to feminine attributes of God and calls God Mother. We have included one such new hymn in our collection. This is another issue you may care to discuss in your groups.

How the Material was Chosen

Over a period of a year a small group supported by a wider group of consultants (see Appendix I) met to plan this course. They sang together, shared their responses to the music, honed and whittled until they came up with the selection you now have. This is not a comprehensive selection and there are many gaps. While we acknowledge the rich diversity of religious music, including organ, choir and instrumental music, we have chosen to focus our selection on *participatory singing*. The songs, worship songs and hymns presented here will be supplemented by the material that members of your group bring each week. The material in the body of the course includes music from the mainstream Christian traditions, from Britain and Ireland, music from outside these islands, religious music and folk music, solo pieces and congregational pieces, Orthodox liturgies, and texts that reflect different theological perspectives. We have ordered the pieces according to the date when the words were written, beginning each week with the oldest and working through to the most recent.

The Gospel readings are taken from Year B of the Revised Common Lectionary. Churches are increasingly using a Common Lectionary (a scheme of planned Bible readings). Years A, B and C all have a variety of readings attached to them. Lent 2000 falls in Year B, the appropriate extract of which is given in Appendix II.

The Rhythm of Each Week

Each week begins with suggestions for worshipping together, following the Gospel reading for that week. After the Gospel reading, each week we have provided an imaginative reflection, *'through the eyes of'* one of those who encountered Jesus, which is designed to help people relate the Gospel passage to the theme for that week. This is followed by an opportunity to share songs, with or without a religious theme, that have been important to us in our own lives. These songs should be chosen each week by two volunteers from your group (for the first week the leader will have to approach two group members). The middle section of the weekly course will then offer seven songs, chants, worship songs and hymns : people are encouraged to listen to and sing through any that the group feels drawn to. Each one is introduced in the accompanying brief notes and can be heard on the CD. A few broad questions for discussion then follow focused on the week's theme. There will then be a time for shared hospitality and discussion followed by a brief closing worship. The session ends with some ideas for action which can be followed through by the group or in the intervening week. We also offer you a link paragraph if you or your congregation is using the 'Partners in Learning' material (see end of Introduction for more details).

II Practicalities

Ways of Using the Material

The material has been prepared for use in the following ways:

● Small Group

This material is designed to work in a small group of eight to twelve people and can be followed through from beginning to end, bearing in mind the needs of the group, the **Suggestions for Group Leaders** (see pages 13-14), and the flexibility to adapt the pattern and the timing as already indicated.

● Large Group

You may prefer to meet as one large, town/city/village/area-wide group for this course. The course could be followed through as one large group, worshipping and singing together, which will then need to break up into smaller groups for discussion and sharing, coming back together again for the sharing of hospitality and the closing liturgy. If you have a 'Churches Together' group or 'Council of Churches' in your local area, this might be the best place to begin planning a Large Group gathering for Lent 2000.

Whether you are meeting in a large or a small group, these are some of the questions you will need to address:

Planning Group (particularly for a large group)

Who is in it? How far in advance are you meeting? Is it ecumenical? Are there local musicians who can help/who would be comfortable leading a large group in singing songs, some of them new songs, together? How many meetings will you have? What are the key tasks for the group?

Advertising (particularly for a large group)

What kind of advertising do you need? Who will circulate posters/flyers? Are there other forms of advertising (local radio, local press)? Who will liaise with these? How far in advance does this liaising need to happen?

Group Leaders

If you meet as one small group or break up into small groups, who will lead the group, one or more people? Could volunteers be invited to lead the worship/other parts of the session?

Meeting Place

Where will you meet? Will it be the same place each week? Is there enough space for your group? Is there adequate heating/lighting/power points? What about layout of the room and chairs? Can they be arranged in a circle which is usually the most conducive shape for sharing?

Equipment

Do you have a CD player? If not, can you borrow one? Do you have a Bible? Do all members of your group have access to a copy of the material? How many CDs do you want for your group?

Singing

How will your group feel about singing together?

Refreshments

Who will prepare them and will you need a budget? N.B. For some, Lent is an important time for fasting, for re-assessing what we consume in terms of food and material goods. So you may like to reflect on fasting and on what you are 'giving up' or 'taking up' for Lent. While you are sharing refreshments each week you might like to reflect together on fasting.

Flow of the session

If you are meeting in a small group, we suggest that you begin the first session with introductions of group members and then flow straight into the Opening Worship.

Central Focus

Each week a number of symbols are suggested if you want to use a central focus to stimulate reflection or discussion.

Volunteers

Near the beginning of each session two members of your group are invited to share a song or piece of music which has been significant for them at a certain time in their lives. This does not need to be a religious piece of music or song, although that is fine also. **For a small group:** for week 1 the group leader will need to ask for volunteers before the session. For subsequent weeks volunteers can be invited in advance from the group. **For a large group:** as you are meeting in a large group, either these volunteers will need to feel comfortable sharing with the large group, or you could move this section to the beginning of the section on questions for discussion which takes place in small group. You will have to find an appropriate way of nominating volunteers depending on the size of your large group. For week 1 volunteers will need to be invited before the session. For subsequent weeks volunteers can be invited from the group(s) itself/themselves.

Organising a 'Songs of Praise' or 'Big Sing' event

You might like to plan a big celebration in a **'Songs of Praise' or 'Big Sing'** style before the Lent course begins. This could be a wonderful opportunity to learn some of the songs and to introduce the themes of *All Together Now* to a large group of people from all over your town/city/village/area. It could also draw in people who would not normally attend a Lent course. This could be organised by a 'Churches Together' grouping or an ad hoc group of churches coming together for this purpose.

Points to be considered in the planning include:-

i) **Date and Time** - the Sunday evening before Lent (5th March 2000) may be ideal for some; or a week-night evening or other significant day around that date. If it is a Sunday it would be an opportunity for churches to combine their worship services for this occasion rather than hold services at the same time.

ii) **Venue** - What is the most accessible church or venue in terms of transport? What about disability access and acoustics? Which has the size to accommodate the large numbers who may wish to come? Which has the best resources for leading congregational singing? - Or might a joint choir might be formed for this purpose?

iii) **Organisation and Publicity** - a small group representing the churches involved could be delegated to do this - and to clarify who has the responsibility for leading the celebration, introducing the hymns and songs, and leading the music. The planning for this could begin before the end of 1999.

iv) **Content** - this is an obvious opportunity to explain the *All Together Now* course that is about to begin, and to emphasise that thousands are taking part all over the UK. The hymns and songs could be chosen from the material suggested in this book, so that the evening could become a preparation for the journey of Lent. The occasion could reflect the ways different congregations approach Lent and the journey to Easter; or it could give opportunity for individuals to introduce hymns and songs reflecting their own spiritual journey and experiences. It could be an opportunity to sing old favourites, but also to introduce some new material, including some from this course. It might be helpful to practice with the congregation any unfamiliar material beforehand.

v) **Recruiting for the Course** - those attending the celebration need not be confined to those already committed to the *All Together Now* course: it could be a general celebration for your locality. Some people may already have 'signed up' to share in *All Together Now*; others could be encouraged to add their names to any groups that have already been organised, at the end of the celebration. This Lent

Course provides a unique opportunity to invite organists, musicians and choir members to take part, for instance by spreading them around the groups to help with the music and singing. Thus a wider range of people than the regular 'house group attenders' may be drawn in. The celebration would be an opportunity to have copies of this book and the accompanying CD on sale. Socialising over a cup of tea or coffee at the end of the celebration may be very valuable: people may be able to find out more about the course and sign up for it.

vi) You may also like to organise a **Post-Easter Gathering** which could take place on Easter day evening, or looking towards Pentecost. Separate celebrations are being planned in some parts of Britain and Ireland for Pentecost 2000 which you may like to look towards. For further details of Pentecost 2000 contact the national ecumenical bodies (see Appendix IV).

● **Daily Personal Reflection.**

Seven worship songs and hymns, from a variety of traditions and cultures, have been chosen for each week of Lent so that individuals can use this material for personal reflection on a daily basis if they wish.

● **Sunday Worship During Lent**

If you are a worship leader you may like to use the worship songs, hymns and themes offered here during Sunday worship to guide you and your congregation through the Sundays of Lent.

III Suggestions for Group Leaders

Leading a group is a skill which takes practice and wisdom but which can be learned and developed. A good group leader is someone who enables group members to participate fully in the group work and does not, themselves, become the constant focus of attention or reference point. The following suggestions are offered to group leaders:

1. Introductions

Each time you meet in a small group make sure that at or very near the beginning each participant has a chance to say who they are and perhaps a little about themselves. This not only helps us to remember names, but it also gives everyone the chance to hear their voice in the group, which may be a new experience for some people and may also give them confidence for later sharing. It is not enough, therefore, for the leader to go round naming each member of the group. It is a good idea to repeat these introductions each week, to remind ourselves of the names and perhaps to share something slightly different about ourselves. There may be some people in the group who do not belong to any one Christian tradition or may indeed be questioning their faith at its very roots, or be at the beginning of their faith search. It is important that there is no pre-judging of group members and that each person is welcomed for who they are rather than because of where they belong or what they do.

2. Group Guidelines

There are perhaps five basic guidelines to which the group should agree:
i) **Listening:** when someone speaks no-one else interrupts
ii) **Respect:** all ideas and contributions are respected. (This does not exclude sensitive, respectful challenge.)
iii) **Freedom:** we have the freedom to say as little as we like.
iv) **Owning:** speak from your own experience rather than on behalf of anyone else (eg 'everyone surely knows 'Praise my Soul...' ' when in fact some of the group may not).
v) **Confidentiality:** anything of a personal nature that is shared in the room will not be shared outside the room.

There may be other guidelines which the group wishes to establish.

3.   Time-Keeping

There are guidelines for how long you might want to spend on each section although these are not intended to restrict you and you may develop your own pattern which suits the needs of your group. Set a time for the meeting to begin and end and try to keep to it. If, for any reason (eg a discussion takes longer than you thought) it becomes clear that you will end early or late, check out with the group if this is OK and re-schedule accordingly.

4.   The Use of Silence

For some, silence is comfortable. For others the use of silence is a new experience and can feel uncomfortable. If you intend to have spaces for silence during the sessions, perhaps in the opening and closing worship, you could bear in mind the following:

i) Be clear about why you want to use silence. Is it simply to fill in a gap, to offer a token gesture to those who like silence or think it is a good idea, or is it because you are aware of the power of silence to unite a group and to draw us closer to God?

ii) If you suggest time for silence, then do leave a good space. Count to 30, at least. Silence in some churches lasts no more than 4 or 5 seconds!

iii) Offer some suggestions for what your group may like to focus on in the silence, eg the theme of this session, one word, a question, a candle, a symbol.

iv) Make it clear that you or the leader of that section will give an indication when the silence is over, maybe by starting to sing a chant, or to read a short passage. This will allow those who are nervous to rest assured that the silence is being 'held'.

v) Make it clear that silence does not exclude all noise, so we can be aware of the noises around us, and we must not be afraid to make a noise, blow our noses or to cough.

5.   Using the Music

In addition to ensuring that the group has appropriate resources for hearing and singing the music offered and chosen (CD, piano, other instruments, unaccompanied singing) the group will need to be helped to learn, sing, or sing along with the hymns and songs. Either the group leader or group members with appropriate skills can undertake this task. Perhaps there is an opportunity here to invite organists, musicians and members of local church choirs to join different groups and help with the singing. N.B The full music for the hymns and chants in the Opening and Closing Worship are printed within these sections. The material for each week includes the titles and details of each of the seven hymns, songs and chants on each theme, together with references to hymn books where the full music version may be found (The key to abbreviations used for hymn books and song books is in Section IV of this Introduction). The words and melody line for each musical item are printed together within each week's material.

Evaluation

We welcome your feedback. Please send us your comments and constructive criticisms about this course by completing and returning the Feedback Form which you will find in Appendix IV at the end of this book.

Partners in Learning

Partners in Learning is an all age worship resource devised by an ecumenical group for the use of groups and churches based on the pattern of the Christian year. The theme chosen for Lent 2000 in Partners in Learning is 'All this for love', reflecting both on our love for God, and God's love for us. This material provides all-age worship resources for the first five Sundays of Lent to complement the ideas being explored in *All Together Now*.

For further details of Partners in Learning contact:
Partners in Learning Distribution, 1020 Bristol Road, Selly Oak,
Birmingham B29 6LB
tel: 0121 472 4242 fax: 0121 472 7575

IV Hymn Books and Song Books

The following hymn books and song books are referred to by these acronyms in the material for each week as the places where full music versions of hymns and songs may be found.

AMN   Hymns Ancient and Modern New Standard, 1983
BBC   BBC Songs of Praise
BHA   Hymns and Songs for Worship (Brian Hoare), 1986
BHB   Baptist Hymn Book, 1991
BPW   Baptist Praise and Worship
CG   Common Ground
CH   Church Hymnary (3rd Edition) 1973
CP   Congregational Praise 1951
GC   Gather Comprehensive, GIA/Decani
GTG   Glory to God, 1994
HCF   Hymns and Congregational songs Vol 12/3
HP   Hymns and Psalms
HTC   Hymns for Today's Church
LP   Let's Praise (2) 1994
MP   Mission Praise
NEH   New English Hymnal, 1986
NMP   New Mission Praise, 1986
ONA   Hymns Old and New (New Anglican Edition), 1996
ONN   Hymns Old and New (RC New Century Edition) 1994
ONR   Hymns Old and New (RC Edition) 1989
RS   Rejoice and Sing
S   The Source
SH96   Spring Harvest 1996
SH99   Spring Harvest 1999
SL   Sent by the Lord, (Wild Goose Pubs)
SS   Story Song
WGR   When Grief is Raw, (Wild Goose Pubs)
WOV   With One Voice (Australian Hymn Book) (Inc. Catholic Supplement), 1979

Lent 2000

Weeks 1 –5

WEEK 1 Beginnings

Aim: *To explore our beginnings, looking both at the beginning of creation and the beginnings or source of our own faith journey.*

Preparation: You will find Suggestions for Group Leaders on pages 13-14.

1. Timing

The times offered for each section are only suggestions.

2. Volunteers

Before this session two members of the group should be invited to bring with them a piece of music which is important for them from their early memory. This can be a song, a nursery rhyme, an excerpt of music or a sound track from a tape/CD. It does not need to be an explicitly religious piece of music, although that would also be fine. During this session they will be invited to share this piece of music with the group and to say a few words about why it is important for them.

3. Preparation for week 2

In preparation for week 2, two members of the group could be invited to bring for next week a song, hymn or piece of music which was meaningful for them at a time of decision-making in their lives. As with week 1, this does not need to be an overtly religious piece of music or song. Next week they will be invited to share this song or piece of music with the group and to say why it is important for them.

4. Images for a Central Focus (to stimulate discussion or reflection)

Seeds, a snowdrop (see closing prayer), a nappy, images from childhood, confirmation or baptismal certificates.

5. Group Guidelines

At or near the beginning of this session it could be helpful to agree, with the group, the guidelines that you would like to follow (see page13). In subsequent weeks, if there are new group members, these guidelines may need to be revisited.

6. Introductions and Ice Breakers

You may like to incorporate introductions into the Opening Worship if you are working in a small group, or at the point for small group discussion if you are working in a large group. When the group arrives give each member time to introduce themselves by saying a little about who they are. As a focus, you may like to ask members to say, along with their name, one other thing about themselves, or tell you their favourite song of the moment.

1. Opening Worship   (suggested time 10 - 15 minutes)

*Welcome

This could include 'Introductions' as above or it may be a brief sentence of welcome or a short prayer, or a time of silence (see page 14).

Song

We walk by faith, and not by sight – words Henry Alford – music Shanti (Marty Haugen) *This song recognises that we must rely on faith during our life's journey. It is valuable to reflect on where in today's world we can touch the wounded body of Christ. The American Marty Haugen is one of the most popular composers for the Roman Catholic Church though he himself is Lutheran.*

Opening Prayer

Loving God, walk with us on our journey
as we enter a time of reflection and sharing together.

Holy God, kneel with us in our humility
as we acknowledge those times when we have lost sight of you.

Welcoming God, embrace us with your open arms
as we, strangers and friends, find a space here to call our own.

Living God, open our eyes and our hearts
to those excluded from groups, left out of society, abandoned and lonely.

Life-giving God, in Jesus Christ you offer us new hope for our lives and the life of the world, and in the Holy Spirit you promise us companionship and compassion always. May we, in our lives, show hope, compassion and friendship to all around us. Through our time here together may we learn more deeply about who we are and so learn more clearly about who you are, alive in each one of us.

Amen

Psalm (to be sung or read)

O God, you search me and you know me.*

The psalms provide a human response to life's many and varied experiences. Their power has not diminished since the time of their compilation. Jesus and the New Testament writers often drew on them. They also became a major part of monastic devotion in both eastern and western traditions. This setting of psalm 138 (or 139 depending on which version you use) by Bernadette Farrell has a simplicity which allows it to become memorable.

(N.B. THIS PORTION BETWEEN THE ASTERISKS INCLUDING WELCOME, SONG, OPENING PRAYER AND PSALM WILL BE REPEATED EACH WEEK)

WE WALK BY FAITH

SHANTI

Marty Haugen

We walk by faith and not by sight no gra-cious words we hear of him who spoke as none e'er spoke, but we be-lieve him near.

Verse 5 to Coda We may not *Coda* near.

We may not touch his hands and side,
nor follow where he trod;
yet in his promise we rejoice,
and cry "My Lord and God!"

Help then, O Lord, our unbelief,
and may our faith abound;
to call on you when you are near,
and seek where you are found:

That when our life of faith is done
in realms of clearer light
we may behold you as you are
in full and endless sight.

We walk by faith, and not by sight:
no gracious words we hear
of him who spoke as none e'er spoke
but we believe him near.

Henry Alford (1810-1871) alt.

O GOD, YOU SEARCH ME

Based on Ps 139   Bernadette Farrell

O God, you search me and you know me. All my thoughts lie o-pen to your gaze. When I walk or lie down you are be-fore me: ev-er the

mak - er and keep - er of my days.

You know my resting and my rising.
You discern my purpose from afar,
and with love everlasting you besiege me:
in ev'ry moment of life or death, you are.

Before a word is on my tongue, Lord,
you have known its meaning through and through.
You are with me beyond my understanding:
God of my present, my past and future, too.

Although your Spirit is upon me,
still I search for shelter from your light.
There is nowhere on earth I can escape you:
even the darkness is radiant in your sight.

For you created me and shaped me,
gave me life within my mother's womb.
For the wonder of who I am I praise you:
Safe in your hands, all creation is made new.

Gospel Reading

Mark 1:9-15

Reflection : to be read aloud

Through the eyes of John the Baptist
Some people think that it all began with me, that there was something that I said or did to Jesus when I baptized him which prompted him to start on the journey which would change so many lives - including his own. But it wasn't like that at all. It had begun years before I stood there in the waters of the Jordan and the people came to me searching for new beginnings in their own lives.

Something happened when Jesus came out of the water, something that went back to the dawn of creation itself. Perhaps it was the rippling of the waters and that flash of sudden light from the skies which was too bright to gaze upon. Water and light: they were the elements out of which God had made our world. Now they were being used again to mould a new creation, a new beginning for our world. The water was washing away the grime of the centuries. And when Jesus stood there in the water it was as though all the power of God to create, to renew, to make a new world was focussed in him. Heaven and earth somehow met that day - and nothing that has happened since has been able to tear them apart again.

I realised that day just how powerful love can be: that voice from the skies called Jesus God's beloved. Love can bring about a whole new way of living, and that is what Jesus came to tell people. He understood that so much better than I did! After our meeting at the river Jordan he went out into the desert to fight off all that the powers of evil could throw at him - and he was victorious. Then he came back and he walked around the villages of Galilee - sweeping away the cobwebs in people's hearts and souls and challenging them to begin again.

Prayer

either Lord, give me such a longing for you and for your ways that I can never cling to anyone, or anything else, as though it were my ultimate security. **Amen**

or a prayer of your own choosing

2. Sharing the Words and Music   (suggested time 20-30 mins)

1. Give the two group members who have brought a song or a piece of music with them the chance to share that with the group, spending up to 5 minutes each explaining why the piece of music is important to them.

2. Look through the list of songs for this week. Listen to or sing through any that the group members feel drawn to. They are all to be found on the CD which accompanies this course. The group leader may like to select one or two in order to get the group started. N.B. Each hymn or song, melody and words, is printed with the material for each week. The notes about them which follow here and at the same point each week also indicate where full music versions may be found in a number of hymn books. The key to the abbreviations for these hymn books is in Section IV of the Introduction on page 16.

1.   Be thou my vision   words: Mary Byrne music: Slane
This hymn is found in two 8th century Irish manuscripts. Mary Byrne translated it into prose in 1905. Eleanor Hull put it into verse in 1912. It was put into four line verses for the Irish Church Hymnal of 1919 and has since been recast to reach its familiar form. It retains what many feel to be a spirit of Celtic prayer, especially sung to the strong Irish tune SLANE. It is a prayer that looks forward on the Christian's way and seeks the varied gifts that will be needed.
CH 87, HP 378, HTC 545, MP 51, ONA 56, ONN 53, RS 489, S 50, WOV 455.

2.   Amazing Grace   words: John Newton music: trad.
John Newton came to faith only after some years as master of a ship in the slave trade. In 1779 he published with William Cowper a collection of hymns for his parish of Olney. Here in a fine hymn of evangelical faith he speaks of the beginning of that faith, but also of the continual help of God on his way through life. One reason why this hymn has become popular in the British and Irish churches is that the tune (an American folk-tune, probably based on a Scottish melody) was included in a recording of music for bagpipes.
BBC 282, BHA 25, BPW 55, HP 215, HTC 28, MP 1, ONA 27, ONN 31, RS 92, WOV 56.

3.   To Christ the Seed   Irish Traditional
This traditional song comes from a people connected to their environment - to the land and the sea. The theme of beginnings was very important in rural culture. Farming and fishing folk were well aware of the potential harvest locked up in seed and spawn. The same sort of potential, for growth development, is alluded to in the reference to human birth and a new life after death.
CG 135

4.   Lord, you give the great commission   words: Jeffery Rowthorn music: Abbot's Leigh
This hymn is by a Welshman who has moved to the USA and is a bishop in the Episcopal (Anglican) church. It can be used as a hymn for an ordination or the commissioning of a minister. The words of Jesus in the second line of each verse can be applied to all church members, to challenge us to prayer and action and to Christian hope, to the new commitment that each Lent asks for.
RS 580

BE THOU MY VISION

SLANE   Irish traditional melody

Be thou my vi - sion, O Lord of my heart,

naught be all else to me, save that thou art -

thou my best thought in the day and the night

wak - ing and sleep - ing thy pre - sence my light.

Be thou my wisdom, be thou my true word,
thou ever with me and I with thee, Lord;
thou my great father, thy child let me be,
thou in me dwelling, and I one with thee.

Be thou my breastplate, my sword for the fight;
be thou my dignity, thou my delight,
thou my soul's shelter, and thou my strong tower;
raise thou me heav'nward, great Power of my power.

Riches I heed not, nor earth's empty praise,
thou mine inheritance, now and always;
thou and thou only, the first in my heart,
High King of heaven, my treasure thou art.

High King of heaven, thou heaven's bright sun,
grant me its joys after vict'ry is won;
heart of my own heart, whatever befall,
still be my vision, O Ruler of all.

Ancient Irish poem tr.Mary E Byrne (1860-1931) and Eleanor H.Hull (1860-1935) altd.

AMAZING GRACE

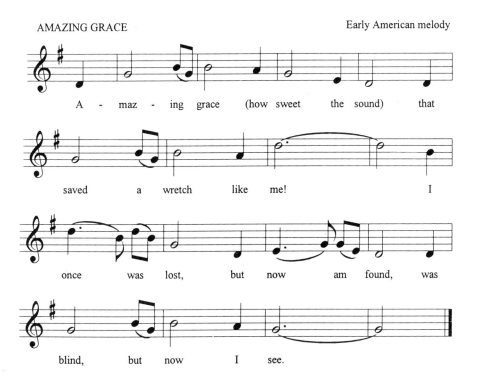

AMAZING GRACE   Early American melody

A - maz - ing grace (how sweet the sound) that

saved a wretch like me! I

once was lost, but now am found, was

blind, but now I see.

Through many dangers, toils and snares
I have already come;
God's grace has brought me safe thus far,
and he will lead me home.

The Lord has promised good to me,
his word my hope secures;
he will my shield and portion be
as long as life endures.

And, when this heart and flesh shall fail
and mortal life shall cease,
I shall possess within the veil
a life of joy and peace.

John Newton (1725-1807) alt.

TO CHRIST THE SEED

IRISH TRADITIONAL   Sean O'Riada

To   Christ the seed to   Christ   the sheaves: so

in - to God's barns   may   we   all   be brought.   To

Christ the   sea;   to   Christ   the   fish: so

in - to God's nets   may   we   all   be caught.   From

birth   to   growth,   from   growth   to   age   may your

two   arms, O Christ,   fold   us   a - round.   From

age   to death,   from   death   to new birth   in   the

pal - ace of grace may we be found.

Ag Criost an siol;	To Christ the seed;
ag Criost an fornhar.	to Christ the sheaves:
In iothlainn De	so into God's barns
go dtugtar sinn.	may we all be brought.
Ag Criost an mhuir;	To Christ the sea;
ag Criost an t-iasc.	to Christ the fish:
I lionta De	so into God's nets
go gcastar sinn.	may we all be caught.
O fhas go haois,	From birth to growth,
is o aois go bas,	from growth to age
do dha laimh, a Criost,	may your two arms, O Christ,
anall tharainn.	fold us around.
O bhas go crioch,	From age to death,
ni crioch ach athfhas,	from death to new birth
i bParthas na nGrast	in the palace of grace
go rabhaimid.	may we be found.

Anon

tr. JW from 'Common Ground'

THE GREAT COMMISSION

ABBOT'S LEIGH

Cyril V. Taylor

Lord, you give the great com - mis - sion:

'Heal the sick and preach the word'.

Lest the Church neg - lect its mis - sion

and the gos - pel go un - heard,

help us wit - ness to your pur - pose

with re - newed in - teg - ri - ty;

with the Spi - rit's gifts em - power us

for the work of min - is - try.

Lord, you call us to your service:
'In my name baptize and teach'.
That the world may trust your promise,
life abundant meant for each,
give us all new fervour, draw us
closer in community;
with the Spirit's gifts empower us
for the work of ministry.

Lord, you make the common holy:
'This my body, this my blood'.
Let us all, for earth's true glory
daily lift life heavenward,
asking that the world around us
share your children's liberty;
with the Spirit's gifts empower us
for the work of ministry.

Lord, you show us love's true measure:
'Father, what they do, forgive'.
Yet we hoard as private treasure
all that you so freely give.
May your care and mercy lead us
to a just society;
with the Spirit's gifts empower us
for the work of ministry.

Lord, you bless with words assuring:
'I am with you to the end'.
Faith and hope and love restoring,
may we serve as you intend,
and, amid the cares that claim us,
hold in mind eternity;
with the Spirit's gifts empower us
for the work of ministry.

Jeffery Rowthorn (1934 -)

OUT OF DARKNESS

Christopher Walker

REFRAIN

Out of dark-ness God has called us, claimed by Christ as God's own peo-ple.

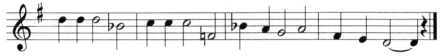

Ho - ly na - tion, roy - al priesthood, walk-ing in God's marv'-lous light.

VERSES

Let us take the words you give. Strong and faith-ful words to live.
Let us take the Christ you give. Bro - ken Bo - dy, Christ we live.
Let us take the love you give, that the way of love we live.

Words that in our hearts are sown; words that bind us as your own.
Christ the ris - en from the tomb; Christ who calls us as your own.
Love to bring your peo - ple home; love to make us all your own.

GOD HAS CHOSEN ME

Bernadette Farrell

VERSES:

God has cho - sen me, God has cho - sen me to
God has cho - sen me, God has cho - sen me to
God is call - ing me, God is call - ing me in

bring good news to the poor. God has cho - sen me, God has
set a - light a new fire. God has cho - sen me, God has
all whose cry is un - heard. God is call - ing me, God is

cho - sen me to bring new sight to those search - ing for light: God has
cho - sen me to bring to birth a new king - dom on earth: God has
call - ing me to raise up the voice with no pow - er or choice: God is

REFRAIN:

cho - sen me, cho - sen me: And to tell the world that God's
cho - sen me, cho - sen me:
call - ing me, call - ing me:

king dom is near, to re - move op - pres - sion and break down fear, yes God's

time is near, God's time is near, God's time is near, God's time is near.

YOU KNOW ME

Mike Stanley

Sensitively

You know me, you formed me, you gave me life.

From dark - ness you called me, you changed my life. And

ev - en as the sun sinks down, I see your light shine through. For

still the stars of hea - ven shine and I'm a - live in you, a - live in

you. You know me, you formed me, I'm a - live in you,

a - live in you. You know me, you formed me,

I'm a - live in you, a - live in you.

You know me, you heal me, you set me free.
You opened up your arms and gave your life for me.
And though the skies were darkened
And the Heavens torn apart,
For love your life had ended,
That in truth my life may start, my life may start.

You know me, reach out and take my emptiness.
Transform me and let me share your holiness.
Though clouds may gather round me
When you seem so far away;
Mould me in your image
As the potter moulds the clay, moulds the clay

You know me, I know you, we are as one,
The old life has ended, the new begun,
For in the silent moments
In the sunrise, in the fields,
All creation sings in praise
And so you are revealed, you are revealed.

5.　　Out of Darkness　　　　　　　　words and music: Christopher Walker

This song represents a strong call to service and mission which is the duty of all Christians. The refrain is taken up by the whole assembly and the verses are sung by the cantor or choir. Christopher Walker was for 18 years Director of Music at Clifton RC Cathedral. He now works in America as a composition lecturer, liturgical musician, composer and workshop leader.
GC 689

6.　　God has chosen me　　　　　　　words and music: Bernadette Farrell

In his Gospel, Luke records one moment in history when a reader in a small synagogue stood up and proclaimed the words of the prophet Isaiah. And the world changed. Today, through our calling, we share in the mission of Jesus Christ. Bernadette Farrell's vibrant song can be delivered in unison with verses sung by cantor or in the easily learned harmonies provided.
GC 682 LP 276, NMP 32

7.　　You Know Me　　　　　　　　words: Mike Stanley arrangement: Chris Rollinson

Inspired by Jeremiah 1 : 5 this song speaks of the transforming and life-giving nature of Jesus' love, a love necessarily expressed through sacrifice. The composer Mike Stanley works alongside Jo Boyce heading up CJM Music, a company committed to serving the Church through the ministry of music.

3. Questions for Discussion　　　　　　　(suggested time 30-40 mins)

(you may like to focus on one or two)

1.　　If you were to write a song about the beginning of your own faith journey, what words and/or images would you use?

2.　　You may like to explore your experiences of: calling - vocation - ministry - being chosen. In what way do these experiences indicate a 'new beginning' on the journey of faith?

3.　　Do any phrases, words or images from the songs selected for this week stand out for you? If so, why?

4. Sharing hospitality　　　　　　　(suggested time 15-20 minutes)

Continue discussion over refreshments. (See page 10 for notes on refreshments).

5. Closing Worship (suggested time 5 minutes)

N.B. For large groups breaking into small groups
If you have been in small groups up until now and are coming together to worship, one or more of these chants could be being sung as people gather.
N.B. Music for Closing Worship is on pages 39 onwards.

Take O take me as I am
God knows us better than we can ever know ourselves. This quiet song of dedication can be sung a number of times as the group gathers for worship, setting a tone of openness and reflection
Ubi Caritas
Veni Creator Spiritus

During the singing of the chant a symbol from the session might be brought into the worship space. Before the prayer there could be a short time of silence.

Prayer

either:

Into a dark world
a snowdrop comes
a blessing
of hope and peace
carrying with it
a green heart
symbol of God's renewing love.

Come to inhabit our darkness
Lord Christ,
for dark and light
are alike to you.

May nature's white candles of hope
remind us of your birth
and lighten our journey
through Lent and beyond.
                    Amen

from 'The Pattern of Our Days' Wild Goose Publications

or a prayer of your own choosing

Closing song or chant:

either:

Night has fallen

This beautiful evening song is one of a number of hymns from Central Africa brought to Europe and the USA by a Scottish missionary. It may be sung in harmony, unaccompanied, or melody only - the last syllable of the refrain being held on as the solo begins the next verse.

or

The day thou gavest Lord is ended

This hymn was written towards the end of the 19th century when people were beginning to think of the British Empire as that on which the sun never sets. John Ellerton took this same notion and applied it to the Church and to the Kingdom of God. However, its popularity was due to Queen Victoria's choosing it for Jubilee services, and thereby opposing too much triumphalism (v.5) .

or

Jesus Remember Me

This closing worship will be repeated each week but with a different prayer for each session.

Ideas for Further Action

1. Are there any small projects in your area which you would like to support and which are struggling to get started, to make a new beginning? You could offer your support.
2. Introduce yourself to a visitor who is beginning to come to your Church.
3. Pray for a different neighbour this week.

N.B. Don't forget Preparation for Week 2 (see pages 10 and 18).

Partners in Learning link for Week 1

The words spoken by God to Jesus at his baptism include 'In you I take delight'. Delight is an exuberant word, full of emotion, and far from simply being a pallid warm feeling! This week the Partners in Learning theme asks what is 'Love's Delight'. Appropriately we use some sacred songs to help us in this task.

TAKE, O TAKE ME AS I AM

John L. Bell

Take, O take me as I am;
sum - mon out what I shall be;
set your seal up - on my heart and live in me.

UBI CARITAS

Jacques Berthier

U - bi ca - ri - tas et a - mor

u - bi ca - ri - tas De - us i bi est.

VENI CREATOR SPIRITUS

Jacques Berthier

Ve   ni   Cre - a   tor   Spi - ri - tus.

CW4

NIGHT HAS FALLEN

DZUWA LAPITA   Trad. boat song adapt. Tom Colvin

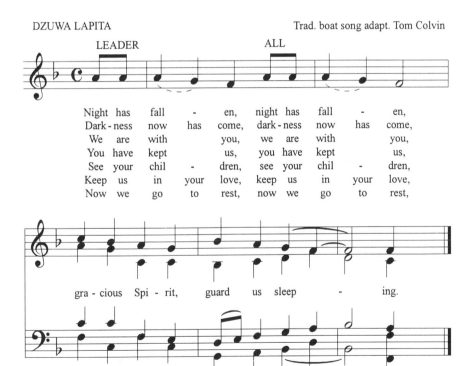

LEADER				ALL			
Night has	fall	-	en,	night has	fall	-	en,
Dark - ness	now	has	come,	dark - ness	now	has	come,
We are	with		you,	we are	with		you,
You have	kept		us,	you have	kept		us,
See your	chil	-	dren,	see your	chil	-	dren,
Keep us	in	your	love,	keep us	in	your	love,
Now we	go	to	rest,	now we	go	to	rest,

gra - cious Spi - rit,   guard   us   sleep - ing.

THE DAY THOU GAVEST

ST.CLEMENT   C.C.Scholefield (1839-1904)

The day thou gav - est, Lord, is end - ed, the
dark - ness falls at thy be - hest; to
thee our morn - ing hymns as cend - ed, thy

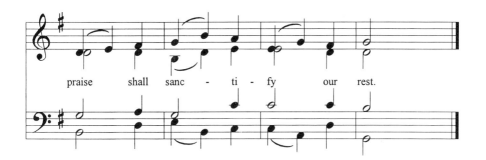

praise shall sanc - ti - fy our rest.

We thank thee that thy Church unsleeping,
while earth rolls onward into light,
through all the world her watch is keeping,
and rests not now by day and night.

As o'er each continent and island
the dawn leads on another day,
the voice of prayer is never silent,
nor dies the strain of praise away.

The sun that bids us rest is waking
our friends beneath the western sky,
and hour by hour fresh lips are making
thy wondrous doings heard on high.

So be it, Lord; thy throne shall never,
like earth's proud empires, pass away;
thy kingdom stands and grows for ever,
till all thy creatures own thy sway.

John Ellerton (1826-93) altd.

43

JESUS, REMEMBER ME

Jacques Berthier

Je-sus, re - mem-ber me when you come in-to your King dom.

Je-sus, re - mem-ber me when you come in-to your King-dom.

© Ateliers et Presses de Taize

WEEK 2 Following

Aim: *To reflect on what it means to follow in today's world: to follow an inner calling, a particular career, a spiritual path, a guru or a holy person.*

Preparation: You will find Suggestions for Group Leaders on page 16.

1. Timing

The times offered for each section are only suggestions.

2. Volunteers

At the end of the last session you should have identified two volunteers who will bring to this session a piece of music from a time of decision-making in their lives.

3. Preparation for week 3

In preparation for week 3, two members of the group could be invited to bring a song or piece of music which helped them through a time in their life when they were offering a challenge or were being challenged. This may be a song which focuses on anger and frustration or more broadly on the theme of challenge. As with last week this can be a song, an excerpt of music or a sound track from a tape/CD. It does not need to be an overtly religious piece of music, although that would be fine also. Next week they will be invited to share this piece of music with the group and to say a few words about why it is important for them.

4. Images

Club membership card, shepherd's crook, photo of a pop star, guru, holy person.

5. Introductions and Ice Breakers

You may like to incorporate introductions into the Opening Worship if you are working in a small group, or at the point for small group discussion if you are working in a large group. Start with a reminder of people's names, particularly if there are new members of the group present. You may like to use the following question: Can you name a TV series/pop group/band you like to follow regularly, and say why in a couple of sentences?

1. Opening Worship (suggested time 10-15 minutes)

Please refer to the section between the * * beginning on page 19. The gospel reading and prayer for this week are given below:

Gospel Reading
Mark 8:31-38

Reflection on the Gospel : to be read aloud

Through the eyes of Peter

If I had realised that first day when I met him by the lakeside just where 'following' Jesus would lead me, I am sure that I would never have dared to begin. I sometimes wonder whether, if we had caught more fish the previous night, Andrew and I would have been prepared to take our chances with this stranger who challenged us to join him. But it had been a lousy night, and the fish had not bitten. I was fed up and wanted a change.

Following is rather like that. You only realise when you are on the journey how much further there is to travel and what twists and turns might lie ahead. When you follow Jesus you learn as much about yourself as you do about him.

I thought I had 'arrived' that day when I discovered exactly who Jesus was. It had taken me and the others a long time, as we followed Jesus round Galilee. I think Jesus was getting exasperated by how slow we were to catch on. Then one day near Bethsaida he healed a man who was blind, and suddenly I too saw, saw clearly for the first time. Jesus had to be the Messiah - the one we were looking for, the one who would make all our age-old dreams come true.

I thought I had 'arrived', but really it was only the beginning. Almost straight away I put my foot in it once again. Because now Jesus started to tell us more, things we didn't want to hear - about suffering instead of glory, about a Messiah who was going to be crucified and whose followers had that road to travel as well. I didn't want to hear. I thought that if I stopped him talking about it then perhaps it wouldn't have to happen. We could take another route together.

What he said next cut me to the quick. Of all the things he said to me in all the years I knew him - this was what I would never forget. 'Satan', he called me. Yet I still continued to follow. Because once you have set out on your journey with Jesus, you can never really look back and pretend that he is not there.

They called those of us who were Jesus' friends his 'followers'. It was a good description - though sometimes he was striding out so fast and so far ahead of us that it felt as though we were travelling into the unknown.

Prayer: (said by all)

either **God, change my ways of seeing, so that in every experience I can recognise you beckoning me to be at one with you and with all creation.** **Amen**

or a prayer of your own choosing.

2. Sharing the Songs   (suggested time 20-30 mins)

1. Give the two group members who have brought a song or a piece of music with them the chance to share that with the group, spending up to 5 minutes each explaining why the piece of music is important to them.

2. Look through the list of songs for this week. Listen to or sing through any that the group members feel drawn to. The group leader may like to select one or two in order to get the group started.

1.   O Jesus I have promised   words: JE Bode music: Wolvercote
Many will associate this hymn with their baptism, confirmation or admission as a church member. Indeed the hymn was written for the confirmation of the author's children. Our theme of 'following' comes out in the repeated 'follow' in the final verse. We can look back and see how true this hymn has been of our way through life and how we still need to pray its words as we look forward.
AMN 235, CH 434, CP 447, HTC 531, NEH 420, ONA 372, ONN 303, S 391, WOV 514

2.   Take my life and let it be   words: FR Havergal music : Nottingham
Frances Ridley Havergal was in frail health all her life, but worked hard in study and in writing. After a conversion experience at the age of fourteen she longed and prayed for the conversion of those around her. After a number of days when such prayer had been richly answered, unable to sleep she renewed her own dedication as a follower of Christ in these lines.
AMN 249, BPW 358, CH 462, CP 458, HTC 554, ONA 464, ONR 510, WOV 520

3.   Weaver-God, Creator   words: Kate Compston music: Noel Nouvelet
The imagery of God as a weaver has emerged as a quite common theme in contemporary hymn-writing and liturgy, and is linked with European and American women's revival of domestic arts such as quilt-making. Kate Compston is a writer of hymns and prayers based in Gosport, and is a minister of the United Reformed Church.

4.   Sent by the Lord am I   words: Jorge Maldonado music: trad.
The world church offers us many resources for enlivening our faith and our worship. This lively song of commitment to following in the path of Jesus comes from Chile. Through it we are led to recognise that following Jesus demands commitment and action on our part: we have a responsibility to involve ourselves deeply in our 'world of hurt and pain.'
CG 105, LP 399

5.   We pause to give thanks   words: Fred Kaan music: Laudate Dominum
Fred Kaan wrote this hymn for the 10th anniversary service in Hong Kong of the Council for World Mission. It gives thanks for the past and reaches out to a future following 'where God leads us.' It is typical of the author that he speaks both of the fullness of the future with God, but also of the realistic risk involved in being a follower in 'a world of "not yet"'. RS 569

6.   Will you come and follow me   words: J.Bell and G. Maule music: Kelvingrove
To follow the gospel-path of truth and justice means to 'care for cruel and kind', to 'risk the hostile stare', to 'set the prisoner free', to overcome the fears and prejudices of the world around us so as to bring change both to ourselves and to that world. In this song, set to a well known folk tune, we are summoned by God in Christ to follow this path, with our eyes wide open to the consequences. As with every summons, it means nothing unless we respond. Verse 5 offers us the words with which to respond.
BPW 363, CG 148, ONA 560, ONN 459

7.   I will offer up my life   words and music: Matt Redman
This song, written in 1994, is by one our our leading contemporary writers in the Worship Song tradition. Using a broad range of biblical ideas, it speaks of the writer's (or of the singer's) total surrender to Jesus and grounds this in the saviour's sacrificial death on the cross.
S 265, SH 99 70

3. Questions for Discussion   (suggested time 30-40 mins)
(you may like to choose one or two)

1.   Is it harder to follow Christ in our modern world than in previous times? Are there particular features of modern life that make it more difficult for us?

2.   Are there specific areas where Christians seem to be called to follow Christ, if necessary at a cost, today?

3.   Do any phrases or words from the songs for this week speak to you about 'following' and what it means to you in your life?

4. Sharing hospitality   (suggested time 15-20 minutes)
Continue discussion over refreshments.

O JESUS, I HAVE PROMISED

WOLVERCOTE W.H.Ferguson (1874-1950)

O Je-sus, I have pro - mised to serve thee to the end; be

thou for ev - er near me, my mas-ter and my friend; I

shall not fear the bat - tle if thou art by my side, nor

wan-der from the path - way if thou wilt be my guide.

O let me feel thee near me;
the world is ever near;
I see the sights that dazzle,
the tempting sounds I hear;
my foes are ever near me,
around me and within;
but, Jesus, draw thou nearer,
and shield my soul from sin.

O let me hear thee speaking
in accents clear and still,
above the storms of passion,
the murmurs of self-will;
O speak to reassure me,
to hasten or control;
O speak, and make me listen,
thou guardian of my soul.

O Jesus, thou hast promised
to all who follow thee,
that where thou art in glory
there shall thy servant be;
and, Jesus, I have promised
to serve the to the end;
O give me grace to follow
my master and my friend!

J.E. Bode (1816-74)

TAKE MY LIFE

NOTTINGHAM   Wolfgang Amadeus Mozart (1756-91)

Take my hands, and let them move
at the impulse of thy love;
take my feet, and let them be
swift and beautiful for thee.

Take my voice, and let me sing
always, only, for my king;
take my lips, and let them be
filled with messages from thee.

Take my silver and my gold,
not a mite would I withhold;
take my intellect and use
every power as thou should choose

Take my will, and make it thine;
it shall no longer be mine:
take my heart, it is thine own;
it shall be thy royal throne.

Take my love; my Lord, I pour
at thy feet its treasure store:
take myself, and I will be
ever, only, all, for thee.

Frances Ridley Havergal (1836-79)

WEAVER-GOD

NOEL NOUVELET   French Carol

Wea - ver - God, cre - a - tor, sets life on the loom,

draws out threads of col - our from prim - or - dial gloom.

Wise in de - sign - ing, in the wea - ving deft:

love and just - ice joined the fab - ric's warp and weft.

Called to be co-weavers, yet we break the thread
and may smash the shuttle and the loom, instead.
Careless and greedy, we deny by theft
love and justice joined - the fabric's warp and weft.

Weaver-God, great Spirit, may we see your face
tapestried in trees, in waves and winds of space;
tenderness teach us, lest we be bereft
of love and justice joined - the fabric's warp and weft.

Weavers we are called, yet woven too we're born,
for the web is seamless: if we tear, we're torn.
Gently may we live - that fragile earth be left
with love and justice joined - the fabric's warp and weft.

Kate Compston

SENT BY THE LORD AM I

Source not known

Sent by the Lord am I; my hands are rea-dy now to make the earth the place in which the king-dom comes. Sent by the Lord am I; my hands are rea-dy now to make the earth the place in which the king-dom comes. The an - gels can - not change a world of hurt and pain in - to a world of love, of jus - tice and of peace. The task is mine to do, to set it real - ly free. O help me to o - bey; help me to do your will.

Text: Jorge Maldonado (Chile); Music Arrangement: Copyright © WGRG Iona Community

WE PAUSE TO GIVE THANKS

LAUDATE DOMINUM   C.H.H.Parry

We pause to give thanks and fo - cus our thought on

how far our God his peo - ple has brought. We

pause for af - fir - ming our 'yes' to his call, pur -

su - ing his fu - ture: life's full - ness for all.

The future is here
as Christ sets us free;
we reach out in hope
for all that will be.
We go where he leads us,
to time's furthest ends,
to share in his mission
as partners and friends.

We rise and we risk
the course he has set,
to care for our world,
a world of 'not yet';
at one in the Spirit,
we follow Christ's way
and put into practice
God's future today.

Creator of worlds,
our Future and Source,
all that we are now,
or will be, is yours.
Enlarge our devotion,
as humbly we vow
to bring your tomorrow
to bear on our now!

Fred Kaan

Words © 1989 Stainer & Bell Ltd.

WILL YOU COME AND FOLLOW ME?

KELVINGROVE

Scottish Traditional

Will you come and fol - low me if I but call

your name? Will you go where you don't know and

ne - ver be the same? Will you let my love be

shown, will you let my name be known, will you

let my life be grown in you and you in me?

© 1989 WGRG Iona Community

Will you come and follow me
if I but call your name?
Will you go where you don't know
and never be the same?
Will you let my love me shown,
will you let my name be known,
will you let my life be grown
in you and you in me?

Will you leave yourself behind
if I but call your name?
Will you care for cruel and kind
and never be the same?
Will you risk the hostile stare
should your life attract or scare,
will you let me answer prayer
in you and you in me?

Will you let the blinded see
if I but call your name?
Will you set the prisoners free
and never be the same?
Will you kiss the leper clean
and do such as this unseen,
and admit to what I mean
in you and you in me?

Will you love the 'you' you hide
if I but call your name?
Will you quell the fear inside
and never be the same?
Will you use the faith you've found
to reshape the world around
through my sight and touch and sound
in you and you in me?

Lord, your summons echoes true
when you but call my name.
Let me turn and follow you
and never be the same.
In your company I'll go
where your love and footsteps show.
Thus I'll move and live and grow
in you and you in me.

John Bell and Graham Maule

I WILL OFFER UP MY LIFE

Matt Redman

VERSES

I will of-fer up my life in spi-rit and truth,
You de-serve my ev-'ry breath for You've paid the great cost;

pour-ing out the oil of love as my wor-ship to You.
giv-ing up Your life to death, ev-en death on a cross.

in sur-ren-der I must give my ev-'ry part;
You took all my shame a-way, there de-feat-ed my sin,

Lord, re-ceive the sac-ri-fice of a bro-ken heart.
o-pened up the gates of heaven and have be-ckoned me in.

CHORUS

Je-sus, what can I give, what can I bring

to so faith-ful a friend, to so lov-ing a King?

Sav-iour, what can be said, what can be sung

as a praise of Your name for the things You have done?

Oh, my words could not tell, not ev - en in part

of the debt of love that is owed

by this thank - ful heart.

5. Closing Worship (suggested time 5 minutes)
Silence and chants (see pages 37-38)

Prayer
either:
One: Where Christ walks,
All: **We will follow.**
One: Where Christ stumbles,
All: **We will stop.**
One: Where Christ cries,
All: **We will listen.**
One: Where Christ suffers,
All: **We will hurt.**
One: When Christ dies,
All: **We will bow our heads in sorrow.**
One: When Christ rises again in glory,
All: **We will share his endless joy.**
One: There is no other way,
All: **He is the only way.**

Stages on the Way page 54

or a prayer of your own choosing

Closing Song or chant 2

Ideas for Further Action

1.   Note down what movements or networks you belong to and why are they important to you.

2.   Share your notes with one or two other members of the group.

3.   Visit another group member's church and see how they 'follow' Jesus.

3.   Consider fasting from one meal or a TV programme. What did you do with your time? How does it feel?

Partners In Learning Link for Week 2

'Love's Breadth' is this week's title and topic. There is an amazing and costly inclusiveness to God's love, which we are called to emulate. Readings from the medieval mystic Julian of Norwich help with our exploration and we use two songs based on her writings.

WEEK 3 Challenging

Aim: *To share with each other about times when we have felt challenged or when we have wanted to offer a challenge to those around us, and to reflect on how we have dealt with the feelings, including anger and frustration, that emerged.*

Preparation: You will find Suggestions for Group Leaders on pages 13-14.

1. Timing

The times offered for each section are only suggestions.

2. Volunteers

At the end of the last session you should have identified two volunteers who will bring to this session a piece of music which helped them at a time when they were being challenged or were offering a challenge.

3. Preparation for week 4

In preparation for week 4, two members of the group could be invited to bring for next week a song or a piece of music which sums up a belief they hold dear. As with previous weeks, this can be a song, a hymn, an excerpt of music or a sound track from a tape/CD. It does not need to be an overtly religious piece of music, although that would be fine also. Next week they will be invited to share this piece of music with the group and to say a few words about why it is important for them.

4. Images

Newspaper, radio, symbol of local controversy.

5. Introductions and Ice Breakers

As with previous weeks, where you have Introductions will depend on whether you are meeting in a large or a small group. Start with a reminder of people's names, particularly if there are new members of the group present. You may like to use the following question: Have you ever heard a piece of music that has really challenged you to do something positive to change the world or a particular situation?

1. Opening Worship (suggested time 10-15 minutes)

Please refer to the section between the * * beginning on page 19. The gospel reading and prayer for this week are given below:

Gospel Reading
John 2: 13-22

Reflection on the Gospel: to be read aloud

Through the eyes of Hannah, an old woman of Jerusalem

When I was younger I had a stall in the outer courtyard of the Temple where I tried to make a few coppers from the pigeons I kept in a pile of crates. Passover was coming up soon, and I hoped that trade might be a bit more brisk. My husband had done quite well with the sheep the day before. But everyone hurried past my stall. It was a slow and frustrating day. Then I heard this great commotion from the other side of the courtyard. I looked up and saw him - this Rabbi type.

He wasn't the smooth-talking kind from the city, but one of those from up North; and he had quite a band of followers with him as well. He was sort of running towards me, for he had spotted the large pile of crates on my stall. 'Buy them here, Master' I called out, 'Nowhere cheaper in town.' Without warning, he gave a heave, and over went my crates with a great crash. Several broke open, and off went the birds. Before I could say anything, he was past me, pushing out here and there turning over other people's trestles. You should have heard the rumpus and the swearing. I had had enough. I burst into angry tears, and I was still trying to calm down half an hour later when I made my way through the outer gate. There he was outside, still arguing with the Temple police. 'Haven't you done enough for today?' I shouted at him. 'Not so fast, Sister', he replied. 'You are too quick with your tongue. What is this place? A thieves' market or a House of Prayer?' Well, that was the last straw. How do you feed a family on pious talk? So I stormed home.

That night I argued with Daniel my husband. He said that the Rabbi had made him think. What was the Temple for? We knew what it had stood for in the past, the presence of God among his people. But now, hadn't it become a bit of a mockery? We certainly didn't feel any closer to God there than anywhere else. Daniel spoke the truth, but I didn't want to hear him then.

I nursed my anger against that Rabbi for three long years, and when I heard that his foolish words had finally caught up with him, I went to spit at him as he was led away to justice. He had fallen to the ground just before he reached the corner where I was standing. The weight of the wooden beam he was forced to drag along was just too much. He clambered back on his feet, reeling from a soldier's lash. He nearly stumbled into me. I looked at him, torn between anger and pity. He saw me. 'Still so angry, Sister?' he said. And then he saw my tears, and he smiled at me, wryly and sadly. He was pushed along and then disappeared.

That was when I let go of my anger. But it was a long time before I really knew who that strange man was. Looking for God in a building can make us feel safe and in control. But to find God in a person who argues with you, contradicts you, and turns your world upside down - that is more than most of us expect in a lifetime.

Prayer (said by all)

either **Living Spirit, as we face the challenges of the days ahead, we call on you to be with us. Give us the courage we need to challenge the world around us so that it can become a living sign of your Kingdom. Amen**

or a prayer of your own choosing

2. Sharing the Songs (suggested time 20-30 mins)

1. Give the two group members who have brought a song or a piece of music with them the chance to share that with the group, spending up to 5 minutes each explaining why the piece of music is important to them.

2. Look through the list of songs for this week. Listen to or sing through any that the group members feel drawn to. The group leader may like to select one or two in order to get the group started.

Exploring the Journey of Faith in Words and Music

1.   Arise, O God   words: David Melling/Fr. Ephrem Lash music: traditional from Constantinople
Arise, O God is sung first and then as a refrain after each of the verses of psalm 82 (81). In many Orthodox churches seats are banged and a huge noise made while the singing and reading goes on, so that the Gates of Hell can be heard falling beneath the feet of Christ. As a result, the verses are often virtually shouted. The singers do not wait for the verses to end before crashing in with the refrain once again. This psalm is sung between the Epistle and the Gospel of the Liturgy of the Harrowing of Hell, the ancient Paschal liturgy of the East, now celebrated on Great Sabbath morning (the Saturday in Holy Week). The liturgy celebrates Christ's triumph over death and his raising Adam and Eve and the Just of the ages.

2.   O breath of life   words: Bessie Porter Head music: Spiritus Vitae
We use the word 'Comforter' of the Holy Spirit, often failing to remember that the word originally meant 'Strengthener'. In this hymn we pray, as so often, that the Spirit will 'come', but this time that the coming will unsettle us and make us know our need. The Holy Spirit is the greatest 'Challenger' of all.
HP 777, HTC 237, MP 488, RS 302, S 379

3.   Through all the world   words: Shirley Erena Murray music: Angelus
Shirley Erena Murray works in the heart of Wellington, New Zealand, and in this hymn looks out on a world that is all too familiar from whichever hemisphere we see it. Jesus challenged us to see him in all who are suffering and the author spells that out, challenging us to follow Christ in heart and mind and action into places in our present world where we would normally be reluctant to go.
'In Every Corner Sing'

4.   Inspired by love and anger   words: J. Bell and G. Maule music: Sally Gardens
There are many situations in our lives and in this world which enrage us, which challenge us, which inspire us to action. In this song, set to an Irish folk tune known to many, the challenges of our world are set within the context of a loving God who acts for good. We may vent our rage and frustration on God, but in the end of the day we must be the ones to act on God's behalf (verse 5, which could be sung solo), following the example of the 'saviour without safety' (verse 6). Verses 3 and 4 may be omitted.
CG 63, ONA 252

5.Jesus Christ is Waiting   words: J. Bell and G. Maule music Noel Nouvelet
Jesus is not distant from our world but fully immersed in it, on the streets, 'waiting', 'raging', 'healing', 'dancing', and 'calling'. In our world, through our world, through us he experiences the loneliness and the injustices, the hatred and the suffering which we inflict and which we bear. In this song we cry out to Jesus: 'listen, Lord Jesus', we are with you in the world, we want to follow you through the pain and the suffering. The tune helps keep this song moving, and is a good tune to sing as we follow on the pathway.
BPW 534, CG67, ONA 268, ONN 209

ARISE, O GOD

Tone 7

A - rise, O God, judge the earth, for you shall have an in - he - ri - tance in all the na - tions.

"Arise, O God ..." is sung first and then as a refrain after each of the verses of the psalm.
The verses are read by a single voice.

God stands in the assembly of Gods;
in their midst he will judge gods.

How long will you judge unjustly:
and accept the persons of sinners?

Judge for the orphan and the beggar,
do justice to the humble and pauper.

Rescue the poor and the beggar;
deliver them from the hand of the sinner.

They have neither known nor understood;
they walk in darkness.
Let all the earth's foundations be shaken.

I said: you are gods
and all of you children of the Most High;
but like men you die,
and fall like one of the rulers.

O BREATH OF LIFE

SPIRITUS VITAE   Mary Jane Hammond (1878-1964)

O Breath of life, come sweep - ing through us,

re - vive thy church with life and power;

O Breath of life, come, cleanse, re - new us,

and fit thy church to meet this hour.

O Wind of God, come, bend us, break us,
till humbly we confess our need;
then in thy tenderness remake us,
revive, restore; for this we plead.

O Breath of love, come breathe within us,
renewing thought and will and heart;
come, love of Christ, afresh to win us,
revive thy church in every part.

O Heart of Christ, once broken for us
'tis there we find our strength and rest;
our broken, contrite hearts now solace,
and let thy waiting church be blest.

Revive us, Lord! Is zeal abating
while harvest fields are vast and white?
Revive us, Lord, the world is waiting,
equip thy church to spread the light.

Elizabeth (Bessie) Porter Head (1850-1936)

THROUGH ALL THE WORLD

ANGELUS

Adapt. from melody by G.Joseph
in Heilige Seelenlust

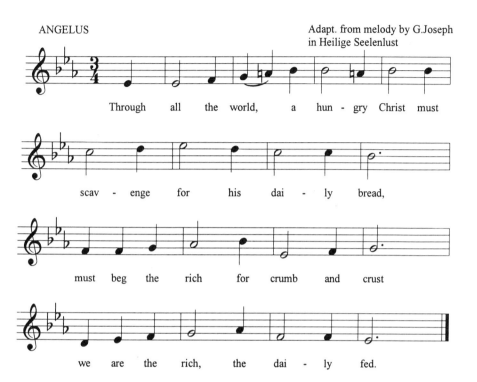

Through all the world, a hun - gry Christ must
scav - enge for his dai - ly bread,
must beg the rich for crumb and crust
we are the rich, the dai - ly fed.

Beyond the Church, a leper Christ
takes the untouchable by hand,
gives hope to those who have no trust,
whose stigma is our social brand.

In torture cell, a prisoner Christ
for justice and for truth must cry
to free the innocent oppressed
while we at liberty pass by.

we do not know you, beggar Christ,
we do not recognize your sores;
we do not see, for we are blind:
forgive us, touch us, make us yours.

Shirley Erena Murray

3.4 INSPIRED BY LOVE AND ANGER

SALLEY GARDENS   Irish folk tune

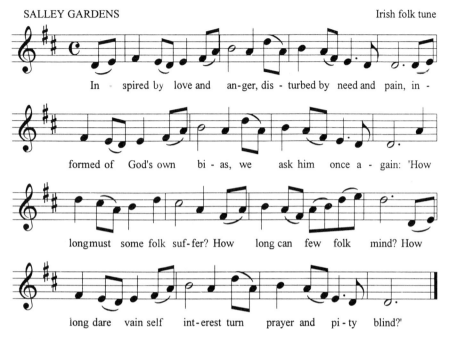

In - spired by love and an-ger, dis - turbed by need and pain, in -

formed of God's own bi - as, we ask him once a - gain: 'How

longmust some folk suf-fer? How long can few folk mind? How

long dare vain self int-erest turn prayer and pi - ty blind?'

1 Inspired by love and anger,
disturbed by need and pain,
Informed of God's own bias,
we ask him once again:
'How long must some folk suffer?
How long can few folk mind?
How long dare vain self interest
turn prayer and pity blind?'

2 From those forever victims
of heartless human greed,
their cruel plight composes
a litany of need:
'Where are the fruits of justice?
Where are the signs of peace?
When is the day when prisoners
and dreams find their release?'

3 From those forever shackled
to what their wealth can buy,
the fear of lost advantage
provokes the bitter cry;
'Don't query our position!
Don't criticise our wealth!
Don't mention those expoited
by politics and stealth!'

4 To God, who through the prophets
proclaimed a different age,
we offer earth's indifference,
its agony and rage:
'When will the wronged be righted?
When will the kingdom come?
When will the world be generous
to all instead of some?'

5 God asks, 'Who will go for me?
Who will extend my reach?
And who, when few will listen,
will prophesy and preach?
And who, when few bid welcome,
will offer all they know?
And who, when few dare follow,
will walk the road I show?'

6 Amused in someone's kitchen,
asleep in someone's boat,
attuned to what the ancients
exposed, proclaimed and wrote,
a saviour without safety,
a tradesman without tools
has come to tip the balance
with fishermen and fools.

66   John L. Bell & Graham Maule

3.5 JESUS CHRIST IS WAITING

NOEL NOUVELET · French Carol

Je - sus Christ is wait - ing, wait - ing in the streets;

no - one is his neigh - bour, all a - lone he eats.

Lis - ten, Lord Je - sus, I am lone - ly too.

Make me, friend or stran - ger, fit to wait on you.

1
Jesus Christ is waiting,
waiting in the streets;
no one is his neighbour,
all alone he eats.
Listen, Lord Jesus,
I am lonely too.
Make me, friend or stranger,
fit to wait on you.

2
Jesus Christ is raging,
raging in the streets,
where injustice spirals
and real hope retreats.
Listen, Lord Jesus,
I am angry too.
In the Kingdom's causes
let me rage with you.

3
Jesus Christ is healing,
healing in the streets;
curing those who suffer,
touching those he greets.
Listen, Lord Jesus,
I have pity too.
Let my care be active,
healing just like you.

4
Jesus Christ is dancing,
dancing in the streets,
where each sign of hatred
he, with love, defeats.
Listen, Lord Jesus,
I should triumph too.
Where good conquers evil
let me dance with you.

5
Jesus Christ is calling,
calling in the streets,
'Who will join my journey?
I will guide their feet'.
Listen, Lord Jesus,
let my fears be few.
Walk one step before me;
I will follow you.

Text: John L. Bell &
    Graham Maule
© WGRG
Iona Community

3.6 LOVE INSPIRED THE ANGER

NORTH COATES   T.R.Matthews (1826-1910)

Love in - spired the   an - ger that   cleared a tem - ple   court,

ov - er - turned the   wis - dom   which their greed had   wrought.

Love inspired the anger
that set the leper free
from the legal strictures
that brought misery.

Love inspired the anger
that cursed a viper's brood:
set on domination,
self with God confused.

Love inspires the anger
that curses poverty,
preaches life's enrichment,
seeks equality.

Love inspires the anger
that still can set us free
from the world's conventions
bringing liberty.

Andrew E. Pratt (1948 -)

I WILL SPEAK OUT

Ray Goudie, Steve Bassett
Dave Bankhead & Sue Rinaldi

I will speak out for those who have no
I will speak out for those who have no

voi - ces, I will stand up for the
choi - ces, I will cry out for

rights of all the op-pressed, I will speak truth and
those who live with-out love, 3 I will show God's com-

jus - tice, I'il de - fend the poor and the need - y, I will
pas - sion to the crushed and bro - ken in spi - rit, I will

3

lift up the weak in Je - sus' name.
lift up the weak in Je - sus'

2   3

name,   in Je - sus' name.

6.   Love inspired the anger   words: Andrew E. Pratt music: North Coates
Jesus may have been 'gentle', but he was not 'meek and mild'! There are many occasions in the Gospels where he is portrayed as very deeply moved or shaken by what he sees and on occasion it is clear that this emotion is anger. Here Andrew Pratt starts with our Gospel reading and points us to some other similar occasions, challenging us to be genuinely angry at some of the things in the world around us.
SS 90

7.   I will speak out   Dave Bankhead et al
There is a Christian calling to stand alongside and support those who are on the margins of the world's societies. This is simply expressed in this song with its evocation of truth, justice and compassion "in Jesus' name."
SH 96 70

3. Questions for Discussion   (suggested time 30-40 mins)
(you may like to choose one or two)

1.   Does the gospel story excite you, frighten you, challenge you, shock you....?

2.   What organisations, institutions or ideologies might be the target of Jesus' anger today? What should Christians challenge in our world today? How do we channel our anger?

3.   Is there one phrase, image or word that stands out for you in the songs selected for this week? Why?

4. Sharing hospitality   (suggested time 15-20 minutes)
Continue discussion over refreshments.

5. Closing Worship *(suggested time 5 minutes)*

Silence and chants (see pages 37 and 38)

Prayer

either

Give us, O Lord, churches
That will be more courageous than cautious;
That will not merely 'comfort the afflicted' but will also 'afflict the comfortable';
That will not only love the world but will also judge the world;
That will not only pursue peace but will also demand justice;
That will not remain silent when people are calling for a voice;
That will not pass by on the other side when wounded humanity is waiting to be healed;
That will not only call us to worship but will also send us out to witness;
That will follow Christ even when the way points to the cross.

Christian Conference of Asia

or a prayer of your own choosing

Closing song or chant (see pages 38 and 42-44)

Ideas for Further Action

1. Is there something which you have felt frustrated about for a long time but have never been able to name? How could you name it in a way that helps you but does not damage others?

2. During the week watch the local news or read a local paper and be aware of the feelings you are having.

3. Pray for one person whom you find it difficult to get on with this week

---

Partners In Learning Link for Week 3

This week the title is 'Love's anger.' We discover that true love can, and sometimes must, burn with the fierceness of anger. Anger can be a powerful force in helping us change the situation of those who are called to love.

WEEK 4 Believing

Aim: *To begin to reflect on and name beliefs that we hold dear. To share these with others in the group and to allow ourselves to be shaped and challenged by the beliefs of others.*

Preparation: You will find **Suggestions for Group Leaders** on pages 13-14.

1. Timing

The times offered for each section are only suggestions.

2. Volunteers

At the end of the last session you should have identified two volunteers who will bring to this session a piece of music which sums up a belief that they hold dear.

3. Preparation for week 5

In preparation for week 5, two members of the group could be invited to bring a song, piece of music or hymn for next week which was helpful to them at a time of grief, death, bereavement or when planning a funeral service. As with previous weeks, this can be a song, an excerpt of music or a sound track from a tape/CD. It does not need to be an overtly religious piece of music, although that would be fine also. Next week they will be invited to share this piece of music with the group and to say a few words about why it is important for them.

4. Images

A bible, a book of holy teachings, a scroll.

5. Introductions and Ice Breakers

As with previous weeks, where you have Introductions will depend on whether you are meeting in a large or a small group. Start with a reminder of people's names, particularly if there are new members of the group present. You may like to use the following question: Is there a piece of music or a song that you have heard of which you could say 'This inspired me'?

1. Opening Worship (suggested time 10-15 minutes)

Please refer to the section between the * * beginning on page 19. The gospel reading and prayer for this week are given below:

Gospel Reading

John 3: [1-13] 14-21

Reflection on the Gospel: to be read aloud

Through the eyes of Nicodemus

I remember that night I went to meet Jesus for the first time. It was very dark. There was no moon. It was a week or so after Passover, when he had created such a stir in the temple. My fellow members of the Jewish Council had been horrified by what he had done - he seemed to be challenging our faith at its very core. But he had been an impressive figure, and brave too, and I wanted to know more. Why had he taken this step which could so easily have resulted in his immediate arrest? I sensed his authority - as soon as I met him I happily addressed him as 'Rabbi' even though I knew he had not studied with the scholars in Jerusalem as rabbis normally did, and as I had done myself.

To begin with he seemed to be talking in riddles. It was as though he was playing with me, teasing me - me with all my learned pretensions. He wanted to shake my securities. I had always had a sense that faith was cut and dried - if only you worked hard enough at it you could be quite sure what you were supposed to believe. But he wasn't having it, with all his cryptic talk about the wind blowing where it wanted to! Faith was not something you could pin down neatly, that was what he was telling me.

But as our conversation continued late into that night I began to see things differently. To know with my heart as well as my head, if you like. Jesus started talking about God sending his only Son... about looking to him to be saved. He still didn't explain fully... who is God's Son? But when I looked at his face, I felt strangely warmed. I didn't want to look away ever again. For I knew that I had found there the salvation and healing that I had been seeking for so many long years.

It must have been hours later, though it only seemed like minutes - for time had stood still while I had been talking with Jesus - I walked away from him to go home but the night didn't seem dark any more. It was as though I had been standing in a pool of light that the darkness could never put out.

Prayer (said all together)

either   Holy God, maker of all that is good, show us the way of goodness;
Holy God, maker of all that is true, show us the way of truth;
Holy God, maker of all this is clear, show us the way of clarity. Amen

or   a prayer of your own choosing.

2. Sharing the Songs   (suggested time 20-30 mins)

1.   Give the two group members who have brought a song or a piece of music with them the chance to share that with the group, spending up to 5 minutes each explaining why the piece of music is important to them.

2.   Look through the list of songs for this week. Listen to or sing through any that the group members feel drawn to. The group leader may like to select one or two in order to get the group started.

1.   We give immortal praise   words: Isaac Watts music: Croft's
For many Christians the answer to the question 'what do you believe?' is summed up in the Trinity: God is Father, Son and Holy Spirit. This is not a cold formula but the expression, as in this hymn, of how our living faith in God is 'Trinity shaped.' We grasp the fullness of God's loving work and purposes for the whole of creation when we begin to grasp the mystery of God, Three in One.
AMN 520, BPW 72, CP 220, HP 18, HTC 11, RS 37, WOV 38

2.   Dear Mother God   words: Janet Wootton music Wings (Sue Mitchell-Wallace)
This congregational hymn draws on images of God from Isaiah 40 : 30 and Deuteronomy 32 : 11 to express our faith in a God who is both motherly and fatherly in caring for us and empowering us. Janet Wootton is a contemporary hymn-writer based in London who uses a wide range of biblical imagery including feminine attributes of God who is addressed as Mother as well as Father. Sue Mitchell-Wallace is based in the United States of America. This hymn was used at the 1998 End of Decade Durham Conference 'Towards the Promised Community'.
HCF 1

3.   And can it be   words: Charles Wesley music: Sagina
In singing this hymn to a popular tune like SAGINA it is all too easy to lose in the general cheerfulness the amazement that Charles Wesley is expressing. He is staggered at the mercy of God ('...it found out me!') and that he is now able fully to believe and put his trust in God.
BPW 328, CH 409, CP472, HP 216, HTC 588, MP 33, ONA 30, ONN 32, RS 366, WOV 138

4.   Firmly I believe and truly   words: J H Newman music: Stuttgart
This hymn, which appears simply to summarize the Creed, appeared first as a death-bed confession of faith in JH Newman's poem 'The Dream of Gerontius'. This is a hymn of believing with passion. It emphasises the need both for the doctrine to give spine to our emotions and for warmth that ignites the teaching.
AMN 186, BHB 133, CH 400, HTC 429, NEH 360, ONN 121, WOV 78

5.   By gracious powers   words: D. Bonhoeffer music: Intercessor
Dietrich Bonhoeffer was martyred by the Nazis in the last weeks of the Second World War. A few months before he had written this meditation for the New Year of 1945. His belief in a loving and sustaining God is complete, though he is able to admit his fear and his awareness of further suffering in store. We do not need to pretend to more courage or confidence in our prayers than we actually have.
BPW 117, RS 486

6.   If you believe and I believe   words based on Matthew 18:19 music: Zimbabwean trad.
Prayer combined with faith can be a powerful tool. In this song from Zimbabwe we are reminded of the power of collective prayer based on shared beliefs. During the fight for independence in what was then Rhodesia, the native people of that country sang this song, substituting 'Zimbabwe' for 'God's People'. If this song is used in intercessory prayer we are invited to substitute the names of other countries, situations or people who are in need of liberation.
SL 72

7.   Wonderful Counsellor   words and music: Chick Yuill
Here we have a song from the Salvation Army tradition with typically positive sounding music. It picks on two of the verses in this week's Gospel reading: the light has come, and God has given us his only son. The song also shows how our passage can be linked to Isaiah, chapter 9. Our theme this week is 'believing' and the song can be seen as a credal statement which voices the content of our belief in Jesus.
NMP 167

4.1 WE GIVE IMMORTAL PRAISE

CROFT'S 136TH   William Croft (1678-1727)

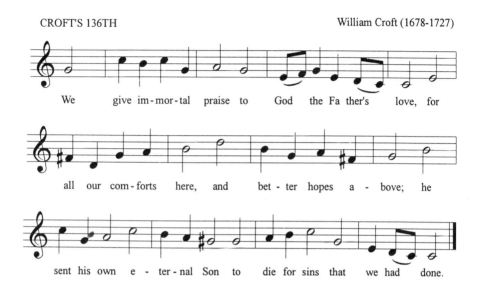

We give im-mor-tal praise to God the Fa ther's love, for
all our com-forts here, and bet - ter hopes a - bove; he
sent his own e - ter - nal Son to die for sins that we had done.

To God the Son belongs
immortal glory too,
who brought us with his blood
from everlasting woe;
and now he lives, and now he reigns,
and sees the fruit of all his pains.

To God the Spirit's name,
immortal worship give,
whose new-creating power
makes the dead sinner live;
his work completes the great design,
and fills the world with joy divine.

Almighty God, to thee
be endless honours done,
the undivided Three,
and the mysterious One;
where reason fails, with all her powers,
there faith prevails, and love adores.

Isaac Watts (1674-1748) altd.

76

DEAR MOTHER GOD

WINGS
Sue Mitchell-Wallace (1944-)

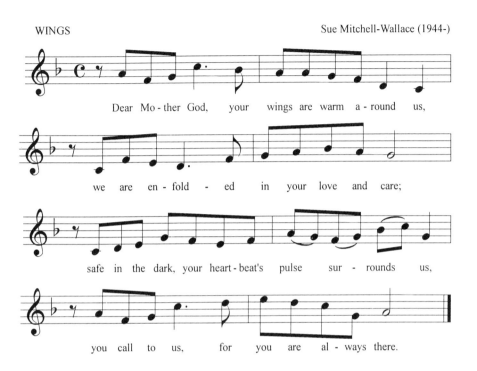

Dear Mo - ther God, your wings are warm a - round us,

we are en - fold - ed in your love and care;

safe in the dark, your heart - beat's pulse sur - rounds us,

you call to us, for you are al - ways there.

You call to us, for we are in your image.
We wait on you, the nest is cold and bare -
High overhead your wingbeats call us onward.
Filled with your power, we ride the empty air.

Let not our freedom scorn the needs of others -
We climb the clouds until our strong heart sings -
May we enfold our sisters and our brothers,
Till all are strong, till all have eagles' wings.

Janet Wootton (1952 -)

AND CAN IT BE?

SAGINA

Published by Thomas Campbell
in his Bouquet (1825)

And can it be that I should gain an

in - terest - in the Sav - iour's blood?

Died he for me, who caused his pain? For

me, who him to death pur - sued?

A - maz - ing love! How can it be that

thou my God, shouldst die for me? A -

maz - ing love! How can it be that

thou,   my   God,   shouldst   die   for   me?

'Tis mystery all: the Immortal dies!
Who can explore his strange design?
In vain the first-born seraph tries
to sound the depths of love divine.
'Tis mercy all! Let earth adore,
Let angel minds enquire no more.

He left his Father's throne above -
So free, so infinite his grace -
Emptied himself of all but love,
And bled for Adam's helpless race.
'Tis mercy all, immense and free;
For, O my God, it found out me!

Long my imprisoned spirit lay
Fast bound in sin and nature's night;
Thine eye diffused a quickening ray -
I woke, the dungeon flamed with light,
My chains fell off, my heart was free,
I rose, went forth, and followed thee.

No condemnation now I dread;
Jesus, and all in him, is mine!
Alive in him, my living Head,
And clothed in righteousness divine,
Bold I approach the eternal throne,
And claim the crown, through Christ, my own.

Charles Wesley (1707-88)

FIRMLY I BELIEVE

STUTTGART   C.F.Witt, 1660-1716

Firm - ly   I   be - lieve and tru - ly   God is Three and   God is One;

and   I   next ac - know - ledge du - ly   man - hood ta - ken   by the Son.

And I trust and hope most fully
In that Manhood crucified;
And each thought and deed unruly
Do to death, as he has died.

Simply to his grace and wholly
Light and life and strength belong,
And I love supremely, solely,
Him the Holy, him the Strong.

And I hold in veneration,
For the love of him alone,
Holy Church as his creation,
And her teachings as his own.

Adoration ay be given,
With and through the angelic host,
To the God of earth and heaven,
Father, Son, and Holy Ghost.

Cardinal J.H.Newman

BY GRACIOUS POWERS

INTERCESSOR

C.H.H.Parry (1848-1918)

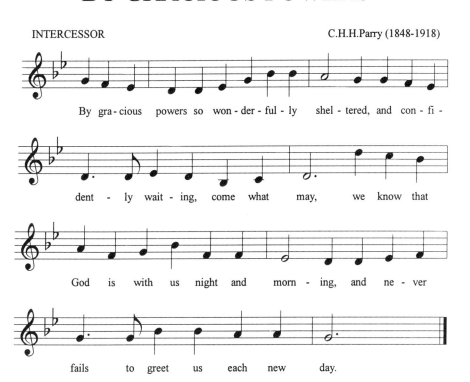

By gra-cious powers so won-der-ful-ly shel-tered, and con-fi-
dent-ly wait-ing, come what may, we know that
God is with us night and morn-ing, and ne-ver
fails to greet us each new day.

Yet is this heart by its old foe tormented,
still evil days bring burdens hard to bear;
O give our frightened souls the sure salvation
for which, O Lord, you taught us to prepare.

And when this cup you give is filled to brimming
with bitter suffering, hard to understand,
we take it thankfully and without trembling
out of so good and so beloved a hand.

Yet when again in this same world you give us
the joy we had, the brightness of your Sun,
we shall remember all the days we lived through,
and our whole life shall then be yours alone.

Dietrich Bonhoeffer (1906-45) (written in prison, for the New Year 1945,
a few months before his execution) Tr. F.Pratt Green (1903-)

IF YOU BELIEVE AND I BELIEVE

Traditional from Zimbabwe

If you be-lieve and I be-lieve and we to-ge-ther pray, the

Ho-ly Spi - rit must come down and set God's peo-ple free, and

set God's peo - ple free and set God's peo - ple free; the

Ho - ly Spi - rit must come down and set God's peo-ple free.

Traditional, based on Matthew 18:19

WONDERFUL COUNSELLOR

Words and music: Chick Yuill

Won - der - ful coun - sel - lor, migh - ty God a - mong us,

ev - er - last - ing Fa - ther, Prince who rules in peace. To

us a child is born, to us a son is given, to

those who walked in dark - ness the light has come.

Son of God, Son of Man,
Word of God incarnate,
suffering Saviour,
glorious risen Lord.
For God so loved the world
He gave his only Son;
no more we walk in darkness
the light has come.

King of kings, Lord of lords,
Son of God exalted;
name above every name,
Lamb upon the throne.
This king will come again,
the Father's only son;
no more a world in darkness,
the light will come.

Chick Yuill

3. Questions for Discussion   (suggested time 30-40 mins)
(you may like to choose one or two)

1.   How would you finish the sentences 'I believe in....' and 'I believe that....'?

2.   In a news programme of 13 April 1999 an anonymous woman from Kosovo, who along with nine others was allegedly raped by Serb soldiers, remarked that it was then that she realised there was no God. How can we respond to this challenge, or understand in any helpful way, the suffering of rape victims, refugees, innocent victims of war?

3.   Do any of the songs/hymns from this week speak to you about believing? In what ways?

4. Sharing hospitality   (suggested time 15-20 minutes)
Continue discussion over refreshments.

5. Closing Worship   (suggested time 5 minutes)
Silence and chants (see pages 37 and 38)

Prayer

either:

One: Come Lord Jesus and sing your song in us
All: that we may live the truth we sing.
One: Show us the path of life and reveal your justice to the nations
All: that we may live the truth we sing.
One: Gently bring us to ways of compassion
All: that we may live the truth we sing.
One: Fill our hearts with the power of your love
All: that we may live the truth we sing.
One: Guide our actions by the light of grace
All: that we may live the truth we sing.
One: Bless us and sustain us in the name of the Trinity
All: that we may live the truth we sing.

from 'Prayer for Parish Groups' page 41

or a prayer of your own choosing

Closing song or chant (see pages 38 and 42-44)

Ideas for Further Action

1.   Think of the times when you have doubted yourself, others, your beliefs/faith. Where has God been in these times?

2.   Share with one other person, in words or by action, how belief in Jesus shapes your life.

3.   Pray for someone you know from a different faith tradition.

Partners In Learning Link for Week 4

This week we explore 'Love's Challenge.' Using the Gospel reading John 3:1-21 we discover that God is like a responsible parent (Mothering Sunday falls on the fourth Sunday in Lent) whose whirling spirit sets us free to take responsibility for our life and actions.

WEEK 5 Dying

Aim: *To explore the meaning of dying and the cross, perhaps offering a new perspective on human death and dying, in the light of our own experience of dying and living.*

Preparation:

Death and dying is a tender issue and will, for some, provoke raw emotions. When preparing for this week, ensure there is enough space in the timetable for safe discussion, while at the same time making it clear that this is not the place for deep hurts and emotions necessarily to be resolved.

You will find **Suggestions for Group Leaders** on pages 13-14.

1. Timing

The times offered for each section are only suggestions.

2. Volunteers

At the end of the last session you should have identified two volunteers who will bring to this session a piece of music, a song, a chant, a hymn which was helpful to them at a time of grief, death, bereavement, or when planning a funeral.

3. Images

Water, grains of wheat, earth, bread, cross, bible

4. Introductions

As with previous weeks, where you have Introductions will depend on whether you are meeting in a large or a small group. Start with a reminder of people's names, particularly if there are new members of the group present. You may like to use one of the following questions:

i) Was there a public death over the last few years that made a particular impact on you? (eg Diana, Princess of Wales, Mother Teresa, images of the dead and dying from Rwanda, Kosovo in the media)

ii) Invite people to mention a song or a piece of music that brought you new vitality when you felt really 'low'.

1. Opening Worship   (suggested time 10-15 minutes)

Please refer to the section between the * * beginning on page 13. The gospel reading and prayer for this week are given below.

Gospel Reading

John 12: [1-8] 20-33

Reflection on the Gospel: to be read aloud

Through the eyes of Mary

Was it what I had done for Jesus only a couple of days beforehand that made him say those words about the seed dying and giving new life? Philip and Andrew tried to tell me that it wasn't - rather it was some people he met at the festival itself who had prompted him to speak about his death. But I will always wonder. Was it because I had anointed him when he came to our house for supper? He looked so tired and so worn that evening. I longed to refresh him in body and soul. It wasn't until I had poured out the ointment and started to wipe his feet with my hair that I remembered that corpses too had precious oils poured upon them - and a chill crept into my soul. I could tell that some of his so-called friends disapproved of what I had done. But Jesus understood - I know he did. He knew that love had to be reckless and extravagant if it was to be worthy of the name. It had to pour itself out completely, empty itself, or else it would never achieve its goal. It is as though you have to die, to offer yourself totally, in order to live again and to give others life.

We had hesitated about summoning Jesus when Lazarus fell sick. Martha and I knew that for Jesus to return to Judaea at that moment was to walk into danger and possible arrest. But somehow he was our only hope. And he came. To give Lazarus life, he was willing even to die. I went to meet him as he arrived. I was weeping and he was moved by my tears. He even wept himself - a man weeping in public! I think that his tears had many meanings. They included compassion for me. They included sadness for himself. I am sure that even then he knew what lay ahead. Yet those tears were also the seeds of resurrection For it is only we who are prepared to sow in tears who will be able to reap with joy.

There was an awful symmetry about Lazarus' resurrection and Jesus' own imminent death. They belonged together. A death for a life, life from the death. Yet I could not feel guilty that Jesus died for my brother Lazarus. For that was his meaning. I truly believe that.

When he spoke of his own death those few days later he was suffering. His soul was in turmoil. And I am glad. There are those who try and tell us that he went gladly and confidently to the fate that awaited him, that he accepted quietly the role that God had for him. They didn't know the Jesus I knew, the one who had wept with me for Lazarus. He was a whole human being, and he suffered as a human being does when faced with death.

Prayer: (said all together)

either

One: The Cross
All: We shall take it
One: The bread
All: We shall break it
One: The pain
All: We shall bear it
One: The joy
All: We shall share it
One: The gospel
All: We shall live it
One: The love
All: We shall give it
One: The light
All: We shall cherish it
One: The darkness
All: God shall perish it. Amen

A Wee Worship Book

or a prayer of your own choosing

2. Sharing the Songs   (suggested time 20-30 mins)

1.   Give the two group members who have brought a song or a piece of music with them the chance to share that with the group, spending up to 5 minutes each explaining why the piece of music is important to them.

2.   Look through the list of songs for this week. Listen to or sing through any that the group members feel drawn to. The group leader may like to select one or two in order to get the group started.

1.   When I survey the wondrous cross   words: Isaac Watts music: Rockingham
In this hymn there is Scripture infused with personal faith and warmth of emotion with an active response that is required from ourselves. In it we are utterly centred on Jesus crucified; we express our emotions, but do not concentrate on them. The response that Isaac Watts proposes for us is the only true one.
HP 180, MP 755, RS 217, S 572 and many others

2.   I cannot tell   words: William Young Fullerton music: Londonderry Air
It is often on Good Friday that the several churches come to worship together, setting aside their differences and admitting their bewilderment at the foot of the Cross. This hymn emphasizes our ignorance, while at the same time expressing our trust in our common Saviour, to the end of life and beyond.
BPW 381, HP 238, HTC 194, ONA 226, RS 265, S 199

3.   Lord Christ we praise your sacrifice   words: Alan Gaunt music: Abingdon
In Alan Gaunt's hymn the key word 'helpless' is in every verse. Before the Cross our normal values are turned upside down. It is very difficult for individual Christians to remember this and even more difficult for churches and their official bodies. This hymn may help us to look at the Cross with new eyes. 'From heaven you came' (No. 5 below) challenges our perspectives in a similar way.
AMN 487, HP 532, HTC 132, RS 611

4.   Unless a grain of wheat   words and music: Bernadette Farrell
The Roman Catholic composer Bernadette Farrell always brings to her music a deep knowledge of scripture and an awareness of its application to people. This song in simple 'responsorial psalm' form is no exception.
GC 697

5.   From heaven you came   words: Graham Kendrick music: The Servant King
This is one of Graham Kendrick's most frequently heard compositions. It attracts by pointing vividly to the paradoxical elements in what God has done in and through Jesus. The king who is the servant enters the world as a "helpless babe" who comes to bear our heavy load, and the "hands that flung stars into space" are surrendered to "cruel nails". Through contemplating this duality, we are to learn to serve and to offer our lives in worship.
BPW 529, MP 162, ONA 148, ONN 130, RS 522, S 114

6.   O Christ you wept   words: J. Bell and G. Maule music: Rockingham
'When Grief is Raw' (Wild Goose Publications, ISBN 0 947988 91 2) from which this song comes is a valuable collection of religious music that deals with the difficulties of bereavement. It does not seek to provide the answers but expresses the pain which Jesus also felt when he learned of the death of Lazarus. Once the pain is laid bare God can start the healing.
WGR p 50

7.   Proclamation of Crucifixion   words: David Melling music: traditional from Constantinople
The Proclamation of the Crucifixion is sung during the service of the Twelve Gospels, the Passion service sung on Great Thursday Night (Maundy Thursday). When it is sung a procession enters the church - which is usually plunged into darkness - the senior priest carrying a crucifix with burning tapers fastened to it, which is set up in the middle of the church, wreathed with flowers and venerated. The priest himself chants the Proclamation on a reading tone while the procession takes place, then the cantors take it up to the melody given.

3. Questions for Discussion   **(suggested time 30-40 mins)**

(you may like to choose one or two)

1.   What music and songs would you like to be played or sung at your funeral?

2.   Have you experienced any particular moments of death and new life in your own living?

3.   It has been said that the church is prepared to do almost anything for God except to die and be reborn. Are there ways in which you think that the church needs to 'die' so that new life can spring up?

4. Sharing hospitality   **(suggested time 15-20 minutes)**

Continue discussion over refreshments.

WHEN I SURVEY

ROCKINGHAM   Adapted by Edward Miller (1731-1807)

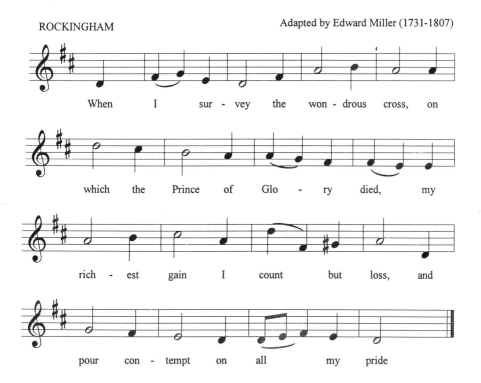

When   I   sur - vey   the   won - drous   cross,   on

which   the   Prince   of   Glo - ry   died,   my

rich - est   gain   I   count   but   loss,   and

pour   con - tempt   on   all   my   pride

Forbid it, Lord, that I should boast
save in the death of Christ my God;
all the vain things that charm me most,
I sacrifice them to his blood.

See from his head, his hands, his feet,
sorrow and love flow mingled down;
did e'er such love and sorrow meet,
or thorns compose so rich a crown?

His dying crimson, like a robe,
spreads o'er his body on the tree;
then I am dead to all the globe,
and all the globe is dead to me.

Were the whole realm of nature mine,
that were a present far too small;
love so amazing, so divine,
demands my soul, my life, my all.

Isaac Watts (1674-1748)

I CANNOT TELL

LONDONDERRY AIR   Irish traditional melody

I can-not tell why he, whom an-gels wor - ship,

should set his love up - on the hu - man race,

or why, as Shep - herd, he should seek the wan-der-ers,

to bring them back with - in the fold of grace.

But this I know, that he was born of Ma - ry,

when Beth-lehem's man - ger was his on - ly home,

and that he lived at Na - za - reth and la - boured,

and so the Sa - viour, Sa - viour of the world, is come.

I cannot tell how silently he suffered,
as with his peace he graced this place of tears,
or how his heart upon the cross was broken,
the crown of pain to three and thirty years.
But this I know, he heals the broken-hearted,
and stays our sin, and calms our lurking fear,
and lifts the burden from the heavy-laden,
for yet the Saviour, Saviour of the world, is here.

I cannot tell how he will win the nations,
how he will claim his earthly heritage,
how satisfy the needs and aspirations
of East and West, of sinner and of sage.
But this I know, all flesh shall see his glory,
and he shall reap the harvest he has sown,
and some glad day his sun shall shine in splendour
when he the Saviour, Saviour of the world, is known.

I cannot tell how all the lands shall worship
when, at his bidding, every storm is stilled,
or who can say how great the jubilation
when all the hearts on earth with love are filled.
But this I know, the skies will thrill with rapture,
and myriad, myriad human voices sing,
and earth to heaven, and heaven to earth, will answer:
at last the Saviour, Saviour of the world, is King!

W.Y.Fullerton (1857-1932)

LORD CHRIST
WE PRAISE YOUR SACRIFICE

ABINGDON

Eric Routley (1917-82)

Lord Christ, we praise your sa - cri fice,
your life in love so free - ly given.
For those who took your life a - way you
prayed, that they might be for - given; and
there, in help - less - ness ar - rayed, God's
power was per - fect - ly dis - played.

Once helpless in your mother's arms,
dependent on her mercy then;
at last, by choice, in other hands
you were as helpless once again;
and, at their mercy, crucified,
you claimed your victory and died.

Though helpless and rejected then
you're now as risen Lord acclaimed;
for ever, by your sacrifice,
is God's eternal love proclaimed:
the love which, dying, brings to birth
new life and hope for all the earth.

So, living Lord, prepare us now
your willing helplessness to share;
to give ourselves in sacrifice
to overcome the world's despair;
in love to give our lives away
and claim your victory today.

Alan Gaunt (1935-)

UNLESS A GRAIN OF WHEAT

INTRO: REFRAIN: Bernadette Farrell

Un - less a grain of wheat shall fall up - on the ground and

die, it re - mains but a sin-gle grain with no life.

VERSES 1-6

If we have died with him
If an - y - one serves me
Make your home in me
If you re - main in me
Those who love me are
Peace I leave with you,

then we shall live with him; if we hold
then they must fol - low me; wher - ev - er
as I make mine in you; those who re -
and my word lives in you; then you will
loved by my Fa - ther; we shall be
my peace I give to you; peace which the

firm we shall reign with him.   Un -
I am my ser - vants will be.   Un -
main in me bear much fruit.   Un -
be my dis - ci - ples.   Un -
with them and dwell in them.   Un -
world can - not give is my gift.   Un -

FROM HEAVEN YOU CAME

THE SERVANT KING   Graham Kendrick

From heaven you came, help - less babe,
There in the gar - den of tears
Come see His hands and His feet,
So let us learn how to serve

en - tered our world, your glo - ry veiled,
my hea - vy load He chose to bear;
the scars that speak of sac - ri - fice,
and in our lives en - throne Him,

not to be served but to serve,
His heart with sor - row was torn,
hand that flung stars in - to space
each o - ther's needs to pre - fer,

and give Your life that we might live. This is our
'Yet not my will but yours,' he said.
to cru - el nails sur - rend - ered.
for it is Christ we're serv - ing.

God, the Ser-vant King, He calls us now to fol-low Him, to bring our

lives as a dai-ly of-fer - ing of wor-ship to the Ser-vant King.

O CHRIST, YOU WEPT

PALMER

John L Bell

O Christ, you wept when grief was raw,
and felt for those who mourned their friend;
come close to where we would not be
and hold us, numbed by this life's end.

The well-loved voice is silent now
and we have much we meant to say;
collect our lost and wandering words
and keep them till the endless day.

We try to hold what is not here
and fear for what we do not know;
oh, take our hands in yours, good Lord,
and free us to let our friend go.

In all our loneliness and doubt
through what we cannot realize,
address us from your empty tomb
and tell us that life never dies.

John L. Bell & Graham Maule

PROCLAMATION
OF THE CRUCIFIXION

Traditional

ALL

To - day is hung up - on a tree, He who hung the earth up - on the

CANTOR

wa - ters. To - day is hung

up - on a tree, He who hung the

earth up - on the - wa ters.

ALL

To - day is hung up - on a tree, He who hung the earth up - on the

CANTOR

wa - ters. To - day is hung up -

on a tree, He who hung the

earth up - on the wa - ters

ALL

To - day is hung up-on a tree, He who hung the earth up - on the

CANTOR

wa - ters. To - day is hung up -

on a tree, He who hung the

earth up - on the wa - ters.

ALL

A crown of thorns is placed on Him, who is the King of the An - gels.

CANTOR

A crown of thorns is placed on Him,

who is the King of the An - gels.

ALL

In false pur-ple He is wrapped, who wraps the hea - vens in clouds.

CANTOR

In false pur - ple He is

wrapped, who wraps the

hea - vens in clouds.

ALL

He re-ceives a blow in the face, He who freed A-dam in the Jor - dan.

CANTOR

He re - ceives a blow in the face, He who freed

A - dam in the Jor - dan.

ALL

With nails is trans - fixed the Bride-groom of the Church.

CANTOR

With nails is trans - fixed the

Bride - groom of the Church.

ALL

With a lance He is pierced, the Son of the Vir - gin.

CANTOR

With a lance He is pierced, the

Son of the Vir - gin.

ALL

We wor - ship your suf - fer - ings, O Christ.

CANTOR

We wor - ship your suf -

fer - rings, O Christ.

ALL

We wor - ship your suf - fer - ings, O Christ.

CANTOR

We wor - ship your suf - fer-ings, O Christ.

ALL

We wor - ship your suf - fer - ings, O Christ.

CANTOR

We wor - ship

your - suf - fer - ings, O Christ.

ALL & CANTOR

Show us al - so Your

glo - ri - ous Re - sur - rec - tion.

5. Closing Worship   (suggested time 5 minutes)

Silence and chants (see pages 37 and 38)

Prayer

either

One: Creator God, out of the depth of your love you called us to new life in Christ. As we rejoice in the resurrection, may our lives and our work together echo the many gifts you have blessed us with for a purpose. May all our being resound with the glory of your name as we say:

All: **Glory be to the Father and to the Son, and to the Holy Spirit, as it was in the beginning, is now, and ever shall be, world without end. Amen**

from 'Prayer for Parish Groups' page 217

or a prayer of your own choosing

Closing song or chant (see pages 38 and 42-44)

Ideas for Further Action

1.   Is there a Hospice nearby which you could support through prayer or action?

2.   Is death or dying something you find easy to talk about with friends or family? Find ways of talking about death with a close friend.

3.   Death can often happen on a massive scale: genocide in the holocaust, in Rwanda, in Kosovo: reflect on how these kinds of mass deaths affect you.

Partners In Learning Link for Week 5

'Love's Passion' is an appropriate title for today, since the fifth Sunday of Lent is often called 'Passion Sunday'. With the gospel reading from John 12 as our guide we marvel at the way love goes to the uttermost, willing even to die for those it loves. The power of love is made known, especially in this moment of apparent weakness.

Appendix I

Members of the Lent 2000 Planning Group

Clare Amos, Partners in Learning
Tony Cheer, United Reformed Church
Lisa Clark, Church of Scotland
Ruth Harvey, Living Spirituality Network (secretary)
Jane Holloway, Evangelical Alliance
Philip Jakob, Roman Catholic Church
Alan Luff, Church in Wales (Anglican)
David Melling, Orthodox Church
Roger Nunn, Churches Together in England (moderator)
Sally-Anne Porter, Scottish Episcopal Church
James Stapleton, Black Christian Concerns Group
Aled Williams, Church in Wales

Consultants to the Lent 2000 Planning Group

Alan Amos, Church of England
Colin Davey, Churches Together in Britain and Ireland
Alec Davison, Religious Society of Friends
Jacynth Hammill, Corrymeela Community
Brian Hoare, Methodist Church
Mary Houston, Churches Together in Britain and Ireland
Diana Murrie, Church of England
James Ozigi, Council of African & Caribbean Churches
David Rudiger, Churches Together in Britain and Ireland
Andy Thornton, Greenbelt Festivals

Appendix II

Extract from Year B of the Revised Common Lectionary (scheme of planned Bible Readings)

First Sunday in Lent   Genesis 9: 8-17
Psalm 25: 1-10
1 Peter 3: 18-22
St. Mark 1: 9-15

Second Sunday in Lent   Genesis 17: 1-7, 15-16
Psalm 22: 23-31
Romans 4: 13-25
St. Mark 8: 31-38

Third Sunday in Lent   Exodus 20: 1-17
Psalm 19
1 Corinthians 1: 18-25
St. John 2: 13-22

Fourth Sunday in Lent   Numbers 21: 4-9
Psalm 107: 1-3, 17-22
Ephesians 2: 1-10
St. John 3: 14-21

Fifth Sunday in Lent   Jeremiah 31: 31-34
Psalm 51: 1-12
or Psalm 119: 9-16
Hebrews 5: 5-10
St. John 12: 20-33

Appendix III

Contact details for national ecumenical bodies

Churches Together in Britain and Ireland (CTBI)
Inter Church House, 35-41 Lower Marsh, London SE1 7RL
tel: 0171 620 4444   fax: 0171 928 0010
e-mail: gensec@ccbi.org.uk   http://www.ctbi.org.uk
General Secretary: David Goodbourn

Churches Together in England (CTE)
101 Queen Victoria Street, London EC4V 4EN
tel: 0171 332 8230/8231   fax: 0171 332 8234
e-mail: any name]@cte.org   http://www.cte-one.clara.net
General Secretary: Bill Snelson

Irish Council of Churches (ICC)
48 Elmwood Avenue, Belfast BT9 6AZ
tel: 01232 663 145   fax: 01232 381737
e-mail: ICPEP@unite.co.uk   http://
General Secretary: David Stevens

Churches Together in Wales (CYTUN)
11 Heol Sant Helen, Abertawe SA1 4AL
tel: 01792 460876   fax: 01792 469391
e-mail: gethin@cytun.freeserve.co.uk
General Secretary: Gethin Abraham-Williams

Action of Churches Together in Scotland (ACTS)
Scottish Churches House, Dunblane, Perthshire FK15 OAJ
tel: 01786 823588   fax: 01786 825844
e-mail: acts.ecu,@dial.pipex.com
http://ds.dial.pipex.com/town/park/geh76/index.html
General Secretary: Kevin Franz

Appendix IV

Evaluation Form

At the end of this course we would be grateful if each group would fill in the following evaluation form and return it to Lent 2000 Evaluation, CTBI, Inter Church House, 35-41 Lower Marsh, London SE1 7RL.

Your answers will be used to evaluate the course and your views will be shared with the Planning Group and the Consultants. It will also be used to inform the group which will plan the next CTBI Lent course in 2002.

In the first eight questions, where the statement is followed by numbers 1-4, please circle:

1   if you strongly agree with the statement
2   if you agree with the statement
3   if you disagree with the statement
4   if you strongly disagree with the statement

Our group met in _____ (name of town, village, city, area)

1.   Theme

    The theme was challenging   1   2   3   4

    The focus on the five different aspects
    of the theme was helpful   1   2   3   4

2.   Worship

    The opening worship helped us move
    into the session   1   2   3   4

    The gospel reflections were helpful   1   2   3   4

    The closing worship was just right   1   2   3   4

3.   The Selection of hymns/songs

We found something there that helped
us each week   1   2   3   4

The selection covered a broad span
of Christian traditions   1   2   3   4

We felt comfortable singing together each week   1   2   3   4

The CD was helpful   1   2   3   4

Group members used the hymns and songs
on a daily devotional basis   1   2   3   4

4.   The Questions

The questions helped us discuss the issues
that were raised each week   1   2   3   4

5.   Ideas for Action

The ideas for action were useful   1   2   3   4

6.   Songs of Praise/Big Sing

These events were well organised and
successful in our area   1   2   3   4

7.   Flow and timing

The flow of each week was helpful   1   2   3   4

We had enough time to get through the material   1   2   3   4

8.   Introduction

The Introduction in general was helpful   1   2   3   4

The Ways of Using the Material was helpful   1   2   3   4

The Suggestions for Group Leaders was helpful   1   2   3   4

9.   Overall impressions

      Our group rated the course as a whole (please circle one number)

      1 (very good)   2 (good)   3 (acceptable) 4 (poor)

10.   If you were to name one feature that was missing from the course what would that be?

      _____

      _____

11.   Your Group

i) Did you meet as a small group or as one large, city/area wide group? _____

ii) How many members were there in your group?_____

iii) Members came from (please circle one number)

1 (one church)   2 (two or more churches)

iii) From which denomination(s) were your group members drawn?

_____

_____

_____

iv) The group (please circle one number)

1 (already existed)   2 (was formed especially for this course)

Members of your group were drawn from the following age groups (please circle each group represented)

under 20   20-35   36-50   51-65   over 65

12.   Local Planning   please circle

          Was there any training for leaders locally?   yes   no

          Were the groups planned ecumenically   yes   no

          Were you pleased with press and media coverage?   yes   no

13.   New Insights

Please identify one new insight or awareness that your group has come to as a result of *All Together Now.*

14.   And finally

Please note either here or on a separate sheet anything else that you would like us to know about *All Together Now.* We are delighted to receive constructive criticism.

ACKNOWLEDGEMENTS

CTBI Publications is grateful to all those who have given permission for copyright material to be reproduced in All Together Now. Every effort has been made to trace copyright owners. An acknowledgement has been placed next to a hymn or song where this has been requested. A complete list of copyright information now follows (full addresses of copyright holders are given the first time they are recorded).

OW: 1	Music © 1984 by GIA Publications, Inc., Chigago, Illinois. All rights reserved. Used by permission.
OW:2	Words and Music © 1992 Bernadette Farrell. Published by OCP Publications, 5536 NE Hassalo, Portland, OR 97213. All rights reserved. Used by permission.
1.1	Words from *The Poem Book of the Gael* © the Estate of the Editor published by Chatto and Windus.
1.3	Words © Church of Scotland Panel on Worship. Used by permission. Music © Riobard MacGovrain.
1.4	Words © 1978 Hope Publishing. Administered by Copycare. Used by permission. Music © Melody by Cyril V Taylor (1907-91) by permission of Oxford University Press.
1.5	Words and Music © 1989 Christopher Walker. Published by OCP Publications. All rights reserved. Used by permission.
1.6	Words and Music © 1990 Bernadette Farrell. Published by OCP Publications. All rights reserved. Used by permission.
1.7	Words and Music by Mike Stanley © 1996 CJM Music Ltd., St Mary's House, Coventry Road, Coleshill, West Midlands, B46 3ED. Used by permission.
CW:1	Words and Music by John L Bell from 'Come All You People' © 1995 WGRG, Iona Community, 840 Govan Road, Glasgow G51 3UU, Scotland.
CW: 2, 3 & 6	Music Jacques Berthier (1923-1994) © Ateliers et Presses de Taizé, 71250 Taizé-Communauté, France. Administered in the UK by Calamus, 30 North Terrace, Mildenhall, Suffolk IP28 7AB. Reprinted with permission.
CW:4	Words and Music © 1969 rev. 1997 by Agape/Hope Publishing Administered by Copycare, PO Box 77, Hailsham BN27 3EF. Used by permission.

4:6   From *Sent by the Lord*, Wild Goose Publications 1991, Words Zimbabwean traditional, Music Zimbabwean variant on an English folk tune arranged by John L Bell © 1991 WGRG, Iona Community.

4:7   Words and Music © Salvationist Publishing & Supplies Ltd., London. Used by permission.

5:2   Words © Baptist Union of Great Britain. Reproduced with permission.

5:3   Words © 1991 Stainer & Bell Ltd.

      Music © Melody by Erik Routley (1917-82) by permission of Oxford University Press.

5:4   Words and music © 1983 Bernadette Farrell. Published by OCP Publications. All rights reserved. Used by permission.

5:5   Words and Music © 1983 Kingsway's Thankyou Music. Used by permission.

5:6   From *When Grief Is Raw*, Wild Goose Publications 1997, Words by John L Bell and Graham Maule, Music by John L Bell © 1996 WGRG, Iona Community.

5:7   Words and transcription and arrangement of music © Archimandrite Ephrem and David Melling.

Prayers and Poems

'Into a dark world a snowdrop comes' from Kate McIlhagga, *The Pattern of Our Days : Liturgies and Resources for worship* © Wild Goose Publications, The Iona Community, Glasgow 1996.

'Where Christ Walks' from *Stages On The Way*, Wild Goose Publications 1998 © 1998 WGRG, Iona Community.

'Give us, O Lord, churches' © Christian Conference of Asia. Source unknown

'Creator God' and 'Come Lord Jesus' from *Prayer for Parish Groups* The Columba Press,1998 © Used by permission.

'The Cross : We shall take it', from *A Wee Worship Book*, Wild Goose Publications 1989, © 1999 WGRG, Iona Community.